Guide to

Patent Policies of Standards-Development Organizations

SECOND EDITION

Jorge L. Contreras, Dave Djavaherian, Christopher Higgins, Jay Jurata, and Emily Luken
EDITORS

AMERICAN BAR ASSOCIATION
Science & Technology Law Section

Cover design by Jill Tedhams/ABA Design

Printed in the United States of America.

26 25 24 23 22 5 4 3 2 1

Library of Congress Cataloging-in-Publication Data

Names: Contreras, Jorge L., editor. | American Bar Association. Section of Science & Technology Law, sponsoring body.

Title: Guide to patent policies of standards development organizations / Jorge L. Contreras, Dave Djavaherian, Christopher Higgins, Jay Jurata, and Emily Luken.

Other titles: Standards development patent policy manual.

Description: Second edition. | Chicago, Illinois : American Bar Association, [2022] | Includes index. | Summary: "This revised edition preserves the structure and intent of the first edition, yet updates it with the results of various judicial decisions, enforcement actions and policy innovations at SDOs around the world. This volume is a useful resource for legal practitioners, judges and scholars seeking to gain a better understanding of this critical area of law and practice, and to serve as a tool for understanding and practice in a complicated legal and technical space"– Provided by publisher.

Identifiers: LCCN 2021062933 (print) | LCCN 2021062934 (ebook) | ISBN 9781639050772 (board) | ISBN 9781639050789 (epub)

Subjects: LCSH: Patent laws and legislation–United States. | Standardization–Law and legislation–United States.

Classification: LCC KF3116.S73 2022 (print) | LCC KF3116 (ebook) | DDC 346.7304/86–dc23/eng/20220202

LC record available at https://lccn.loc.gov/2021062933

LC ebook record available at https://lccn.loc.gov/2021062934

Contents

Preface to the Second Edition

The first edition of this book was published 15 years ago under the title *Standards Development Patent Policy Manual*. At the time, as noted below in the Preface to the First Edition, the American Bar Association (ABA) Section of Science & Technology Law felt that the significant body of case law regarding standards and standards-development organizations (SDOs) warranted a manual to help practitioners understand the policies devised by these important international organizations. It would have been hard to envision what the next decade and a half would bring. Standards-related patent litigation is now occurring around the world—in the United States, Europe, China, Japan, South Korea, India, Brazil, and elsewhere, and parties are embroiled in complex jurisdictional battles that revolve around the meaning of SDO policy terms. Standards-related litigation has taken center stage at prominent international bodies such as the World Trade Organization and the World Intellectual Property Organization, and it figures in the trade policies of major global economies. At the heart of many of these disputes are the SDO patent policies that were first analyzed in the original 2007 edition.

This revised edition preserves the structure and intent of the first edition yet updates it with the results of various judicial decisions, enforcement actions, and policy innovations at SDOs around the world. We hope that this volume remains a useful resource for legal practitioners, judges, and scholars seeking a better understanding of this critical area of law and practice. As with the original draft, this edition does not purport to offer the specific views or policies of any author but rather to serve simply as a tool for understanding and practice in a complicated legal and technical space.

Jorge L. Contreras
Dave Djavaherian
Christopher Higgins
Jay Jurata
Emily Luken

Preface to the First Edition

The project that led to this publication began in late 2003, following the decision of the U.S. Court of Appeals for the Federal Circuit in *Rambus v. Infineon* (318 F.3d 1081). The *Rambus* case involved the interplay between a standard and patents ostensibly needed to implement the standard patents that were owned by a former participant in the standards-development organization (SDO). Prior to this case, many SDOs operated under somewhat informal policies governing disclosure and licensing of such necessary patents. The rules of these organizations were thought to be "understood" by the participants, and in most cases they were.

In its opinion in *Rambus v. Infineon*, however, the Court sharply criticized the patent policy of the SDO in question (the Joint Electronic Device Engineering Council, JEDEC) for its "staggering lack of defining details," which left participants with "vaguely defined expectations as to what they believe the policy requires." The perceived gaps and omissions in the JEDEC intellectual property rights (IPR) policy enabled Rambus to act in a way that was allegedly contrary to the expectations of other SDO participants, but not in violation of the SDO's rules.

The 2003 *Rambus v. Infineon* decision highlighted the need for precision and clarity in SDO intellectual property policies.

Shortly after the decision was published, I discussed with Oliver Smoot, then chair of the Technical Standardization Committee of the ABA's Science and Technology Committee, the initiation of an ABA project to address this issue. This publication is the culmination of that project and includes input from standards experts across industry, academia, and private practice.

The goal of this publication is to provide a resource for SDOs, the lawyers who advise them, and other participants in the standards-development process. It offers a comprehensive set of annotated, policy-neutral language that can be utilized by SDOs who are developing new patent policies and by those who are seeking to refine or interpret existing policies.

This publication is intended to be "policy-neutral"; That is, it does not favor or disfavor particular policy approaches to standards development (for example, whether patents should be licensed on a royalty-bearing or royalty-free basis). Those decisions are left to the SDO and its participants. Rather, this publication seeks to illuminate the legal issues and considerations surrounding such policy decisions, and to help SDOs to implement their policy choices in clear and unambiguous language.

In the interests of both time and brevity, this publication is directed primarily at disclosure and licensing obligations with respect to *patents*. This focus is a result of the significant attention that has been given to patent disclosure and licensing policies in the *Rambus* and other recent cases. This is not to say, however, that the treatment, for example, of copyrights and trademarks within the standards development arena are not worthy of consideration and elaboration. Additional issues such as these may be addressed in subsequent editions of this work.

Jorge L. Contreras
Editor and Chair
Committee on Technical Standardization
Section of Science & Technology Law

About the Editors

Jorge L. Contreras (JD, Harvard Law School; BSEE, BA, Rice University) is a Presidential Scholar and Professor of Law at the University of Utah S.J. Quinney College of Law and the Director of its program on Intellectual Property and Technology Law. Prior to entering academia, Professor Contreras was a partner at the international law firm Wilmer Cutler Pickering Hale and Dorr LLP. His academic research focuses on intellectual property, antitrust law, technical standardization, and science policy. He has published more than 150 academic articles and book chapters and has written or edited 11 prior books including the two-volume set *Cambridge Handbook of Technical Standardization Law* (NY: Cambridge Univ. Press, 2017, 2019). His scholarship has received awards from academic institutions as well as the IEEE Standards Association and the Standards Engineering Society. Professor Contreras has appeared before the US Senate Subcommittee on Intellectual Property, the Federal Trade Commission, and the European Commission. Professor Contreras has served as an expert witness in courts across North America, South America, and Europe, and has lectured in more than two dozen countries around the world. He is an elected member of the American Law Institute and the founding co-chair of the Technical Standardization Committee of the American Bar Association Section of Science & Technology Law.

Dave Djavaherian (JD, Berkeley Law; MA, Georgetown; BA, University of California Berkeley) is a leading international expert on law and policy relating to technical standards and the licensing of standard essential patents. He is president of both PacTech Law, P.C. and PacTech Consulting. His clients include many of the world's largest technology innovators and product companies, as well as many smaller and mid-size technology companies looking to develop and expand their markets. In addition to his legal work, Mr. Djavaherian has been called as an expert witness in several United States and international cases, and served as a delegate for the United States to the United Nation's Telecommunications Standards Advisory Group. He is a regular contributor at standards-development organizations such as ETSI, ITU and IEEE, and is recognized as one of the top 300 intellectury property (IP) strategists in the world. Prior to founding PacTech, Mr. Djavaherian managed in-house legal matters at Broadcom and Tessera. He taught IP Law and Strategy at the University of California, Irvine School of Business, is a Lifetime Fellow of the American Bar Foundation, and a co-chair of the American Bar Association's Technical Standardization Committee.

Chris Higgins (JD, George Washington University Law School; BSEE, University of Cincinnati) is an intellectual property partner at Orrick Herrington & Sutcliffe. He is a trial lawyer with an electrical engineering degree, giving him a unique set of skills to represent clients in disputes involving complex technologies such as graphics processing, semiconductors, medical devices, LCD displays, 3D printing, wireless communication, and data encryption. Chris has represented some of the world's leading technology companies in matters related to standard essential patents and has developed a deep understanding of the inner workings and patent policies of numerous standard setting organizations. In addition to his legal work, Chris is an adjunct professor at Penn State University and teaches a course on legal issues in 3D printing to graduate engineering students.

Jay Jurata (JD, University of San Diego School of Law; BA, Villanova University) leads Orrick Herrington & Sutcliffe's Antitrust & Competition team. A former Surface Warfare Officer in the US Navy, Jay is a Chambers-ranked, first chair trial lawyer and has represented some of the biggest names in business, including Microsoft, Sonos, and Sharp Corporation. Jay has represented both standards-essential patents (SEP) holders and potential licensees in various matters, including a jury trial victory for iBiquity in its SEP licensing dispute with one of its licensees. Jay also is an intellectual property (IP) fellow for the Innovators Network Foundation, and speaks and publishes regularly on topics such as standards-essential patents, fair, reasonable, and nondiscriminatory terms (FRAND), and patent trolls.

Emily Luken (JD, Georgetown University Law Center; BA, Northwestern University) is a Senior Associate in Orrick Herrington & Sutcliffe's Antitrust and Competition team. Emily's practice focuses on issues at the intersection of antitrust and intellectual property, with a particular emphasis on SEPs subject to a commitment to license on fair, reasonable, and nondiscriminatory terms (FRAND). Prior to law school, Emily worked as a research assistant and project coordinator at the Brookings Institution in Washington, DC.

Introduction

Technical interoperability standards are, in many ways, the foundations for modern information exchange, communication, and entertainment. Today, as in the past, governments develop or reference standards to protect the safety, security, and well-being of their citizens. Nongovernmental organizations also develop standards to protect the interests of the public or address a marketplace need. In the past three decades, however, the growth of, and demand for, information and communications technologies (ICT) around the globe have fueled the proliferation of standards developed by industry actors that collaborate within private SDOs.[1] These standards define technical networks, devices, equipment, and interoperability requirements that enable a myriad of products to work together in a growing number of product categories from communications to entertainment to transportation and consumer electronics. This Guide is directed to standards that are developed within such voluntary SDOs and not by governmental agencies.

---

[1] Within the standards arena, the term Standards-Setting Organization (SSO) is often used interchangeably with SDO, each being broad enough to include formal standards bodies, consortia, and special interest groups. The traditional term SDO will be used throughout this Guide.

Nonetheless, this Guide may provide useful information for the development of other types of standards.

THE NATURE AND RANGE OF SDOs[2]

SDOs are diverse in their structure, membership, policies, and objectives, and this Guide attempts to provide a range of options used by SDOs when developing a patent policy or a broader IPR policy that covers patents. This Guide does not endorse any particular policy provision(s) or alternatives; nor does it suggest that included alternatives are exhaustive, applicable, or beneficial for any given scenario. It should be viewed as a starting point at which counsel applies his or her experience and skill.

Many SDOs are incorporated as nonprofit organizations. As such, these SDOs have Articles of Incorporation (or a Charter); these set forth, among other things, the SDO's scope and purpose. Such incorporated SDOs also have Bylaws that describe the SDO's structure and organization, including the composition of the SDO's Board, the duties of the Board members and the Officers of the SDO, the classes of membership in the SDO, and voting requirements and procedures. SDOs often have a membership agreement pursuant to which members agree to follow prescribed terms and to abide by its Bylaws. Such membership agreements may include the processes and procedures employed by the SDO to develop and approve standards. The patent policy, or IPR policy, governing the development, publication, and distribution of the SDO's standards may be part of the membership agreement or part of the SDO's procedures.

---

[2] For a more complete discussion of the legal structures in which SDO IPR policies exist, see Jorge L. Contreras, *A Market Reliance Theory for FRAND Commitments and Other Patent Pledges*, 2015 Utah L. Rev. 479 (2015). and C. Bradford Biddle, *No Standard for Standards: Understanding the ICT Standards-Development Ecosystem*, 1 in Cambridge Handbook of Technical Standardization Law: Competition, Antitrust, and Patents 17 (Jorge L. Contreras ed., 2017).

Members in an incorporated SDO are bound by the terms of the membership agreement with the SDO. Numerous articles and legal decisions have held that both members of an SDO and other implementers of a standard are third-party beneficiaries of the agreement made between other members and the SDO.[3]

Some SDOs are unincorporated, particularly those that are formed to develop a single standard or a very small number of standards. Such SDOs, which are sometimes referred to as consortia or special interest groups (SIGs), often include process and voting rules in their membership agreements since they do not typically have separate Bylaws. The members of an unincorporated SDO are thus bound by these agreements with one another.

In a few SDOs, membership is on a national basis (such as the International Organization for Standardization [ISO], the International Electrotechnical Commission [IEC], and to some extent the International Telecommunications Union [ITU]). Each national body typically organizes or administers the participation of entities or individuals from that nation *vis-à-vis* the technical work at the SDO. This raises additional issues that legal counsel need to take into consideration that are beyond the scope of this Guide.

In some cases, SDOs, both incorporated and unincorporated, have a number of separate patent or IPR policy and procedural documents. For example, it is common for an SDO to have a separate IPR policy governing the development, publication, and distribution of the SDO's standards. Often the procedures used by the Board or other governing body of the SDO

---

3 *See* Contreras, *Market Reliance*, *supra* note 2, at 508–14; Microsoft Corp. v. Motorola, Inc., 696 F.3d 872, 878, 884 (9th Cir. 2012); Realtek Semiconductor Corp. v. LSI Corp., 946 F. Supp.2d 998, 1006 (N.D. Cal. 2013); *In re* Innovatio IP Ventures, LLC Patent Litig., 921 F. Supp. 2d 903, 923 (N.D. Ill. 2013).

to form committees or Working Groups chartered to develop draft standards, and the processes such committees or Working Groups follow to develop standards, are captured in a separate procedural document. Some SDOs develop guidelines such as antitrust guidelines. Typically, the membership agreement references these documents to delineate the expectations of members joining the SDO.

Some SDOs that operate in the United States are accredited by the American National Standards Institute (ANSI) (www.ansi.org), which facilitates the development of American National Standards (ANS) by accrediting the procedures of SDOs. ANSI is not a governmental agency, but rather has served as administrator and coordinator of the United States private sector voluntary standardization system for more than 80 years. ANSI-accredited SDOs work cooperatively to develop voluntary national consensus standards. Accreditation by ANSI signifies that the procedures used by the SDO in connection with the development of ANS that meet ANSI's Essential Requirements for openness, balance, consensus voting, and due process. Accreditation requires that the IPR policy of the SDO be consistent with that reflected in the ANSI *Essential Requirements*. Other SDOs are not accredited by ANSI and have no obligation to comply with the ANSI *Essential Requirements*.

In reviewing the legal aspects of a standard-setting activity, counsel may encounter a wide range of legal issues, including, but not limited to: competition and antitrust issues, corporate formation and governance, contract law, advertising, and intellectual property issues involving patents, copyrights, trademarks and/or certification marks, and trade secrets. Each one of these areas as they relate to standards could be the subject of a separate paper discussing the various choices and the legal, business, and technical ramifications of those choices. This Guide focuses on patent issues.

OPERATION OF THE STANDARDS-DEVELOPMENT PROCESS

Competing suppliers, developers, consumers, and government representatives often come together under the auspices of an SDO to agree upon technical details that form the basis of a standard. Typically, a Working Group or technical committee of the SDO will develop or evaluate a draft standard that describes the technical requirements of the standard, such as a product interface or interoperability protocol. The SDO may then approve or ratify the draft standard as a final standard. Widespread adoption of the standard generally makes it a successful standard, whereas the SDO's policy encouraging the availability of licenses containing reasonable and nondiscriminatory terms and conditions (with or without royalties) to implementers is a factor in making the standard an "open" one.

To encourage such licensing arrangements, most SDOs have a patent policy that defines the nature and trigger for patent license commitments which members of the SDO or contributors to the standards development process are obliged to follow. While patent policies may vary from one SDO to another, it is important for an SDO's patent policy to be internally consistent, evenly and fairly applied, and clear. If this is not achieved, suppliers and consumers may be unsure about the intellectual property risks associated with implementing the standard or using products that support the standard. Also, vagueness and ambiguity can lead to patent holders being uncertain about their obligations, which can further affect the standard.

Participants in the standards process each bring their own unique perspective to a standards activity. Factors such as breadth and depth of patent ownership, degree to which the party intends to implement a particular standard, the subject technology of the standard, the market's expectations, the participant's business model, the participant's technology development model, and a host of other factors influence the desires and perceptions of various standards-setting participants. These factors may also affect a firm differently from one standards activity to another. Therefore, it is important to recognize that each perspective has its own rationale and that the SDO should seek to find an approach that balances its stakeholders' different needs. This can maximize the chances that the resultant standard is the outcome of market-driven requirements, and that it will be successful in the marketplace.

Recently, the number of interoperability standards has greatly increased. With the proliferation of so many standards comes a tremendous surge of competitiveness around the very standards that require so much cooperation to develop. Moreover, unlike other private technology ventures, standards development is generally public in nature, partly because of the large number of parties collaborating to develop a standard and partly due to public interest in the development of quality standards that can be successfully adopted. As a result, there is an ever-increasing awareness of how the IPR policy and processes adopted by a SDO can affect consumers and suppliers.

Standards and Patented Technologies

In general, most SDOs today permit the inclusion of patented technology in their standards. However, SDOs and SDO participants are aware of the potential bargaining leverage that patent holders may obtain if they hold patents covering a broadly adopted standard. This leverage could, under some circumstances, permit a patent holder to extract payments from a potential manufacturer of a standardized product that are in excess of the value of the patented technology itself (i.e., because the standard itself is necessary to a product, and without a license from any one holder of patents covering the standard, the manufacturer potentially could be enjoined, depending on the laws of a particular jurisdiction or the rules of a particular SDO, from implementing that standard in its product).[4]

To avert this threat, many SDOs have adopted different policies and procedures relating to patents. Some SDOs today operate under a patent policy that encourages participants to disclose their patent rights to the extent that essential patent rights would be infringed by practice of the standard. Often participants are expected to license certain patent rights, whether or not those patent rights have been disclosed, under reasonable and nondiscriminatory (RAND) terms and conditions to implementers of the standard. Although RAND is not a precisely defined term in most patent policies, reasonable royalties, field of use restrictions, reciprocity conditions, defensive suspension, and prohibitions on sublicensing as well as many other terms and conditions often appear in standards-related licenses, as discussed further in this Guide.

SDOs and standards implementers invest in the development and adoption of standards by (i) expending time to define a standard, (ii) developing products incorporating the standardized technology, and (iii) basing business plans on the prospective success of the standard in the marketplace. If one of the contributing developers of the standard holds blocking patent rights (meaning the implementer of the standard is unable to obtain a reasonable license under those patents), much of this investment could be wasted. One way that SDOs and standards implementers have tried to avoid this situation is by requiring early disclosure of such patent rights when the patent holder becomes aware that it holds an essential patent claim. Early disclosure of patents is intended to permit participants in the standards development process to choose to incorporate a different technology in a standard if reasonable licenses are not available.

---

4 This threat has been referred to as patent or standards "hold-up," and its prevalence and impact have been debated extensively in the literature.

Ideally, the choice of a noninfringing alternative would avoid future patent infringement litigation between implementers and patent holders. In some circumstances it is easy to remove the infringing technology, while in other circumstances it is not that simple. Since many patent holders may also be implementers of a standard, there is an incentive for them to reduce the need to remove the patented technology.

In the standards context, the selection of an alternative technology to avoid a patented technology may not be a panacea. First, patents are legal documents that should be reviewed and interpreted by a patent attorney. If counsel for multiple participants evaluate the patent rights and alternatives and discuss their opinions, the possible impact on attorney-client and work product privileges should be considered. This type of review can also be costly and take time, although the legal and technical reviews can be conducted in parallel if the SDO has special committees and processes for considering patent questions. Second, in shifting from one technology to another to avoid one patent, it is possible that the alternative selected may also be covered by a patent that is not disclosed either because it is owned by a participant who is not aware of its essentiality or because it is owned by a nonparticipant who is outside of the process and not subject to the SDO's rules and policies.

When a patent is disclosed, an SDO might want to determine if there is a licensing concern before any determinative action is taken (such as selecting an alternative technology). Some SDOs will send a request to the identified patent holder to ascertain whether a RAND licensing commitment is available. Even if the SDO does not receive a reply, however, it is not certain that there will be a licensing issue later because the patent holder may still choose to offer RAND terms or may not pursue patent licenses except defensively. Also, as separate issues, the text of the standard and the scope of any disclosed patent application may change over time, so that an early disclosure may be difficult to make before the final standard is published or before a patent is finally granted. This uncertainty should be factored into the decision whether or not the SDO should seek to design around the patented technology or select an alternative.

In addition, early patent disclosure and "design around" should be considered from a potential infringement perspective. "Intentionally and willfully" infringing or "actively" (knowingly) inducing others to infringe a disclosed patent—whether as part of implementing the standard or other engineering activities—can give rise to additional liability. Accordingly, some companies are reluctant to have their engineers review the details of other companies' patents. A reasonable effort to design around a patent and a competent opinion of non-infringement by patent counsel may help insulate against charges of intentional infringement or inducement to infringe. However, a poorly prepared opinion or no opinion at all may not help. Moreover, a "design around" might still infringe the disclosed patent. When an SDO provides for disclosure of patents and possible "design around" during standards development, the foregoing risks and benefits should be considered, as well as measures to help ensure that effective processes are defined and properly performed.

The question then is the degree to which standards developers and implementers want to make efforts to reduce the risk of future infringement. For SDOs that have a policy that requires early disclosure of patents, there are several trade-offs that warrant consideration in making the decision to design around disclosed patents. For example, is it better to delay establishing the standard by choosing a noninfringing alternative (recognizing that there is no certainty that the alternative does not raise other patent issues) or to try to guard against the possible impact on implementers and the market if there is a chance that implementers are unable to obtain acceptable licenses from nonmembers after the standard is adopted? And is it better to attempt to design the standard so as to avoid a patent, knowing that avoidance activity could potentially raise other costs and legal risks? Each SDO and its participants must evaluate and weigh these concerns on a case-by-case basis when faced with the disclosure of a patent that will not be licensed under RAND terms and conditions.

Thus, a challenge for each SDO is to develop a patent policy that encourages relevant patent holders to join and balances the interests of all its stakeholders: (1) those that contribute patented technology to the development activity, (2) those that make and sell products, and (3) those that use products that incorporate the standardized technology. At a minimum, an SDO should strive to have a policy that is clear and evenly and consistently applied throughout the standards development process and in different international jurisdictions. In addition to having a clear policy, the SDO may also benefit from having a clear process for managing disclosures and for managing the SDO's responses to patent disclosures for the above-mentioned reasons.

How to Use This Guide

This Guide is intended to assist attorneys whose clients are participating in the development of an SDO's patent policy or interpreting or operating under such a policy. In this context, counsel can assess the implications of each alternative provision on the client, whether the client is a patent holder, a participant in the standards development process, the SDO itself, an implementer of the standard, and/or a consumer of a standardized product, and better understand the interests of the client and others involved in the standard development process.

This Guide focuses on identifying the various policy components pertaining to a technical standard. It includes seven sections, each beginning with a high-level discussion and followed by two different subsections of text. The first subsection includes sample policy language, and the second subsection, immediately following, includes commentary on that policy language. The sample language has been derived from existing SDO patent policies and offers users a variety of language options that have been tried and tested by SDOs in the past. Provisions that are bracketed represent options among different policy choices. For example, [must/may be] indicates two choices that the SDO may elect when framing the language of its policy. Commentary accompanies the sample language so that standards developers, participants, and consumers can understand the trade-offs that are made in incorporating certain options and/or foregoing other options.

This Guide is not intended as a scholarly treatise or a work of advocacy. We have made every effort to offer explanations and commentary that are informative, accurate, and neutral. There does exist, however, extensive academic commentary and analysis regarding SDO patent policies.

The remainder of this Guide is organized as follows:

Section I, Definitions, includes definitions of terms commonly found in SDO patent policies. As in all legal documents, the manner in which terms are defined greatly affects the parties' rights and obligations. Different SDOs may define the same or similar terms in different ways. The definitions are also important to help ensure that various stakeholders involved in a specific standard-setting activity have a common understanding of what the policy requires. Capitalized terms throughout this Guide have the specific meaning set forth in Section I.

Section II, General Terms, discusses some general rules that are used by SDOs to render patent policies effective and binding on participants. Section II also addresses how an SDO might resolve situations in which participants have not complied with the its rules. Because different SDOs may be structured and governed differently, it is important that the rules used to bind members and resolve noncompliance issues be appropriate for the particular SDO's structure and governance model.

Section III, Patent Disclosures, describes the composition and format of patent disclosure requirements. The purpose of a patent disclosure policy is, generally, to make known to others the existence of "essential" patent claims that are or may be infringed when a standard is implemented. A disclosure policy should establish who should disclose patents, which patents should be disclosed, when the disclosure should be made, what information should be disclosed, and the format in which disclosures should be made. Again, the specific policy requirements may vary from SDO to SDO, and each policy should ideally be defined to meet the needs of the relevant stakeholders. Many of the variations in disclosure policies that exist today are included in Section III. Some patent policies may allow for parties to opt- out of certain disclosure obligations, exempt parties from obligations to disclose under a range of circumstances, or make exceptions to a policy where disclosure is ordinarily not required at all. Section III also includes provisions and commentary relating to the length of time for which one's obligation to disclose patents may persist and any duty to update one's existing patent disclosure statements.

Section IV, Licensing Commitments and Statements, addresses the composition and format of patent licensing requirements. While patent disclosure involves informing others of the existence of essential patent claims, a licensing policy specifies what rights, if any, a patent holder will/may/should offer to others with respect to "essential" patent claims. Some licensing policies impose a licensing commitment on participants based on specific events, such as joining the SDO or a working group thereof, or upon submitting a technical proposal. Other SDOs require that a patent holder submit a "licensing statement" that includes the patent holder's license commitment when requested by the SDO. Section IV offers numerous alternatives for structuring a patent licensing policy and provides commentary for each alternative so that those developing a policy or those who need to understand an existing policy can better assess the relevant language. Note that this Guide addresses the provisions of SDO licensing commitments; it does not attempt to describe the full terms of a resulting patent licensing agreement, which may include numerous terms beyond those required by the licensing commitment.[5] To assist

---

[5] A number of available resources discuss the details of intellectual property licensing, including JORGE L. CONTRERAS, INTELLECTUAL PROPERTY TRANSACTIONS AND LICENSING: THEORY AND PRACTICE (Cambridge Univ. Press, 2022).

the practitioner, however, samples of such licensing agreements are included in Appendix B.

Section V, Normative and Informative References, deals with the unique issues arising from references to standards published and developed by other SDOs.

Section VI, SDO Actions and Responsibilities, offers some alternatives and options that may be used to define an SDO's responsibilities with respect to the patent disclosure process and the licensing process, such as when an SDO must publish or review patent disclosure statements and/or license statements that it receives. The SDO may also include certain disclaimers in the published standard relating to the patent disclosure and licensing statements that it has received. Several alternative provisions in these areas are provided in Section VI.

Section VII, Other Policy Provisions, discusses additional clauses that are included in SDO patent policies, including express prohibitions on injunctive relief, dispute resolution, and choice of law.

The appendices present supplemental material that may be useful to the practitioner. Appendix A offers considerations for the drafter of standardized SDO disclosure and licensing forms and templates. Appendix B contains a sample licensing agreement for standards-essential patents prepared by the UK High Court (Patents) in the case *Unwired Planet v. Huawei* (2017) and the U.S. District Court for the Central District of California in *TCL v. Ericsson* (2019). Appendix C offers a list of leading SDOs and hyperlinks to their publicly available patent/IPR policies.

We hope that users will find this resource to be of use in formulating, interpreting, and advising clients on SDO policies across a wide range of industries and technologies.

SECTION I

Definitions

Every SDO Policy should include a set of definitions used consistently throughout the Policy. The following defined terms are commonly found in SDO patent policies.

> *An "**Affiliate**" of an entity means an entity that directly or indirectly, through one or more intermediaries, controls, is controlled by, or is under common control with such entity. For the purposes of this definition, the term "control" means ownership of more than fifty percent (50%) of the voting securities of a corporation or other business organization with voting securities.*

This definition is used in the case when an SDO elects to extend its Policy not only to the Participating Organization but also to parent companies, subsidiaries, and sibling companies (under common control) of the Participating Organization.

Some SDOs do not adopt this definition because Participants may be large organizations with multiple affiliates within the corporate family. It is sometimes the case that one affiliate is not in a position to cause another affiliate to act in conformance with or be bound by an SDO policy that is only agreed to by the participating affiliate.

A concern with not including Affiliates is that one member of a corporate family could be a Participant in an SDO and enjoy license rights from other Participants, while another family member that may not need a license holds Essential Claims that it is not required to license. While one family member may not have control over another, other measures (e.g., intercompany agreements) can be used to ensure conformance with the relevant Policy. Thus, it may be prudent to require the highest tier member of corporations under common control to be the participant and to substitute "Subsidiary" for "Affiliate."

Another way to avoid the risk of circumvention of the intent of this Policy is to require Participants to represent (as part of their Participation Agreement or otherwise) that all Essential Claims in patents owned by any member of the corporate family are Controlled by the Participant. See definition of "Control."

> *"**Claim**" means a claim of an issued and unexpired [utility][1] patent, [published/published and unpublished] patent application [2], and any other [claim-based] exclusionary right granted by a governmental authority [3].*

It is advisable to include a general definition of "Claim," as this term is used frequently throughout the Policy and should be given consistent treatment.

If an SDO encourages or wishes to impose baseline disclosure/licensing obligations on its Participants, it may wish to limit the definition of Claims only to issued patents, or to impose this limitation in a related definition (such as "Essential Claims"). SDOs wishing greater disclosure or licensing may wish to include some of the other patent variations described below.

1. *Utility patents.* Utility patents may be distinguished from design patents, which have only limited relevance to most technical standards.

2. *Patent Applications.* Patent applications in the United States (and many other countries) are generally published 18 months after filing. Thus, for the first 18 months after filing, U.S. patent applications are not publicly disclosed. The SDO must decide whether the interest of Participants in maintaining the confidentiality of unpublished patent applications and related trade secrets (which may, in some cases, be required by contracts to which the Patent Holder is a party) and avoiding the possibility of patent interference is outweighed by the benefits of disclosure of potential Claims in unpublished patent applications. Some SDOs may allow the Patent Holder to elect whether it wishes to disclose an unpublished patent application, rather than requiring such disclosure. Some SDOs remain silent on whether "patent application" applies to published and/or unpublished applications and leave it to the discretion of the Patent Holder. Other SDOs may require the Patent Holder to disclose only the existence of the Claim in a patent application and no other detail such as the patent serial number, etc. In any case it is preferable that the Policy clearly state whether or not the definition of Claim includes unpublished patent applications.

   An SDO that wishes to require disclosure and/or licensing of patent applications should be aware that claims in patent applications are transitory. The claims may be changed in scope before issuing in a patent or may not issue at all. Thus, if the SDO requires patent applications to be disclosed, SDO Participants should monitor the manner in which claims change during the prosecution process in order to ensure that their SDO disclosures remain accurate. In addition, as standards under development evolve, it may be difficult to determine whether evolving patent applications apply to the unsettled terms of a standard, and it may be overly burdensome on a Patent Holder to monitor this on a continuous basis.

One of the benefits to the SDO of requiring or encouraging the disclosure of patent applications is to give the relevant Working Groups an earlier awareness of potential patents for which licenses may need to be acquired for implementation of a Standard (as it often takes several years for a patent to issue after the filing of a patent application).

It should be noted that the ANSI *Essential Requirements* do not require the disclosure of patent applications, though ANSI-accredited SDOs are permitted to encourage the disclosure of patent applications. A typical disclosure expectation can be acknowledgment of the existence of application claims that potentially may cover the standard. Another typical disclosure expectation is to reference the section of a standard or proposed standard potentially affected by the application, in each case without specifically disclosing the application itself.

3. *Catch all.* This term may include utility models, invention certificates, design patents, and other patent-like rights issued in jurisdictions throughout the world. It is not intended, however, to include other types of intellectual property such as copyrights and trademarks, which require the consideration of different factors and are not addressed in this manual.

*"**Contributor**" means an Individual Participant that makes a Contribution to the SDO.*

While a Participating Organization may be credited with making a Contribution to the SDO and may be required to disclose and/or license rights with respect to a Contribution, only individuals can actually make a Contribution to the SDO process. This definition is used to identify such individuals. See definition of "***Individual Participant***."

> "**Contribution**" *means any [written] [2] submission to the SDO intended by the Contributor for publication or use as all or part of a Standards Document, [and submitted in accordance with the following Submission Guidelines:] [1].*
>
> *Alternative Options:*
>
> *[and any other statement made within the context of an SDO activity. Such statements include oral statements in SDO sessions, as well as written and electronic communications made at any time or place, which are addressed to an SDO mailing list, session, or SDO management.]*
>
> *[Oral statements shall not be deemed to constitute "Contributions" unless recorded in the minutes of the relevant SDO group and approved in writing by the Contributor within [__] days after the minutes become available.]*
>
> *[Statements made outside of an [SDO] session, mailing list, or other function that are clearly not intended to be input to an [SDO] activity, group, or function, are not Contributions in the context of this Policy.]*

A "Contribution" is an item (whether a technical standard, specification, protocol, design, software code, or methodology, or any portion of any of these) that a Participant submits to an SDO as part of its standards development process. Because an SDO may impose special disclosure and/or licensing obligations for Contributions that are intended to be included in a Standard (see "Mandatory Portion" below), the SDO should consider what types of communications will be considered Contributions.

A "Contribution" to the SDO almost always includes written submissions within the SDO standards process (including written material that is submitted via e-mail, ftp site, posting to a website, or otherwise).

1. In some cases written submissions may need to be in a special format or submitted within specified time frames. The SDO should determine whether any of these requirements is desirable. If an SDO elects to require Contributions to be made formally and in writing, more informal suggestions such as examples or other submissions of technology that may occur during discussions in a standards development session would not be considered "Contributions." In such cases, the SDO should define whether inputs, refinements, alternatives, etc., generated through Working Group activity should be captured. See definition of "***Working Group.***"
2. Some SDOs may also wish for Contributions to include oral statements made by an Individual Participant during a standards development session or on SDO mailing lists as well as documents submitted to the SDO for consideration as a proposal or commenting on a proposal. If an SDO desires to treat such statements as Contributions, it should ensure that it maintains accurate records of the relevant discussions and other communications media (including email archives and written minutes of meetings and/or telephone conferences). In determining whether to allow oral contributions, an SDO needs to balance the administrative burden to the SDO of recording and disseminating accurate minutes with the burden on Participants and possible disruption to the flow of the standards development process of requiring Contributions to be submitted in writing.[1]

---

[1] *See*, e.g., IETF RFC 8179/BCP 79 "Intellectual Property Rights in IETF Technology" Sec. 5.7 (May 2017) [hereinafter IETF IPR Policy], which

*"**Control**" over a patent means ownership of such patent [and/or] [1] the right to grant licenses under such patent to third parties [without such grant resulting in payment of royalties or other consideration to third parties that are not Affiliates] [2] or [provided that if the granting of such license would trigger the payment of any amount to a third-party owner of such patent, then "Control" shall be deemed to exist only if the prospective licensee agrees to make any such payment on behalf of the licensor and otherwise accepts applicable terms set forth in the license agreement] [3].*

The term "Control" is used to identify patents over which a Participant exercises a certain degree of authority, such as ownership or other means of directing its enforcement or licensing. This definition is important because it defines the Essential Claims for which a Participant would be subject to the disclosure and licensing provisions of this Policy.

1. "Control" typically includes patents owned by a Participant (either originally or by assignment, and whether solely or jointly with others). "Control" may also include patents that are owned by a third party, but that a Participant has the right to license. Some SDOs may wish to consider whether a Participant should be deemed to "Control" patents that it owns, but that it is unable

---

includes oral statements as Contributions and requires that "If a Contribution is oral and is not followed promptly by a written disclosure of the same material, and if such oral Contribution would be subject to a requirement that an IPR Disclosure be made (had such oral Contribution been written), then the Contributor must accompany such oral Contribution with an oral declaration that he/she is aware of relevant IPR in as much detail as reasonably possible or file an IPR Declaration with respect to such oral Contribution that otherwise complies with the provisions of . . . above."

to license (due to contractual restrictions or exclusive licenses previously granted, for example). While such situations are not typical, and may be seen as a way for a Participant potentially to circumvent its licensing or disclosure obligations, an SDO that wishes to narrow "Control" in this manner should use "and" in the proposed clause. Otherwise, "or" should be used.

An SDO may wish to address instances relating to Essential Claims Controlled by companies that are owned by several Participants jointly (but in which no one Participant has a majority ownership position). (See Sections III.A.3 and IV.A.1.h.)

2. "Control" is often deemed to exist for inbound patent licenses only if the Participant has the right to grant licenses without incurring any payment or other material obligation to the third-party licensor. This precaution would protect Participants from incurring unexpected royalty obligations when licensing patents as required under this Policy. It could also, however, give Participants an opportunity to encumber patents with royalty obligations in order to avoid obligations under this Policy, though the authors are unaware of instances of such conduct in the standards-setting area.
3. This clause seeks to address the risk identified in [2] above by including all licensable patents within the definition of "Control," but requiring the licensee to bear any payment or other obligations to the third-party patent owner.

*"**Disclosed Claim**" means a Claim that a Participant has previously disclosed to the SDO [in a Patent Disclosure] [1].*

1. Some SDOs that do not have a required form for Patent Disclosures may not wish to include this limitation and may prefer to allow Patent Disclosures to be made in any

form, such as in a Contribution. Many SDOs, however, have prescribed forms for Patent Disclosures, and will not recognize Patent Disclosures unless made in the proper form.

*"**Draft Standard**" means any Standard Document that has been submitted/accepted for consideration as a Final Standard or portion thereof, but that has not yet been [approved/ published] by the SDO in accordance with the SDO's approval process as described in [reference to SDO approval process].*

Where the definition of "Draft Standard" may affect Participant obligations, the SDO should carefully consider which documents are included in this definition. In some cases, an SDO may have numerous levels of classification of Standards Documents, depending on the state of review, approval, and adoption. In some cases, the terms "Proposed Standard" or "Working Draft" may be used.[2] See discussion of "***Final Standard***" below.

*"**Essential Claims**" shall mean all Claims throughout the world that would be Necessarily Infringed (as defined below) by an implementation of a Standard that is compliant with [all][1] Mandatory Portions of the Standard.*

[Optional [2]: Notwithstanding the foregoing sentence, Essential Claims do not include any Claims: (a) other

[2] For example, in the International Standards Organization (ISO), there is a sequence of drafts prepared at different points along the standards development process. At the preparatory stage, there is a "working draft," then a committee (work group) creates a "committee draft," after which a broader inquiry results in a "draft international standard." A final "Draft International Standard" is submitted for approval, and, upon publication, a "Final International Standard" takes effect.

than those set forth above even if contained in the same patent or patent application as Essential Claims; (b) that read solely on any implementations of any portion of a Standard that are not within the bounds of the Scope of the Standard activity; (c) covering enabling technologies that may be necessary to make or use any product or portion thereof that complies with a Standard, but are not themselves expressly required by the Standard.]

The definition of "***Essential Claims***" is one of the most crucial definitions in an SDO patent policy. It is used in two important contexts: (i) determining which patent Claims an SDO may require or encourage a Participant to disclose within the context of SDO activities (see Section III below) and/or (ii) determining Claims for which a licensing commitment is sought (see Section IV below). Note that many SDOs use the term "Necessary Claims" synonymously with "Essential Claims."

It is important to understand that this definition relates only to "Claims," and is thus limited to claims of patents and, depending on the scope of the definition of Claim, patent applications and similar forms of legal protection. It is generally inadvisable to base legal obligations on non-claim language in the patent specification, as those elements do not convey enforceable rights. Moreover, some Claims in a given patent may be Essential Claims and others may not—any obligation should be directed only to Essential Claims and should not include non-Essential Claims, even in the same patent. Thus, use of the term "Essential Patents" is discouraged, unless it is clearly limited to mean the Essential Claims of such patents.

In most SDOs, the Patent Holder generally makes the initial determination whether a Claim is likely to be an "Essential Claim." Most SDOs lack the staff, expertise, and resources to make such determinations, and they expressly disclaim responsibility for identifying or confirming whether a Claim is an "Essential Claim."[3] They must rely on the good faith determinations of their Participants. If a Participant makes such a determination in bad faith or recklessly, then certain remedies may be available to other Participants or implementers of an affected Standard (see Section II.B below).[4]

Global Scope. Including the words "throughout the world" or "in any country" or "worldwide" in this definition reinforces and makes explicit the unlimited geographical scope in which Essential Claims may occur.

Some argue that these geographic words are required explicitly to ensure that the products conforming with a standard can be licensed in other countries where Essential Claims subsist. Other attorneys argue that by omitting any words restricting the geographical scope of the Essential Claims, the geographical scope is unlimited.

Requirement of "Necessary Infringement." This clause is the crux of the "Essential Claim" definition, as it specifies what it means to be "essential." See definition of "Necessarily Infringed."

Mandatory Portions Only. A Standard often contains Mandatory Portions that are required to be implemented for

---

3 *See* e.g., IETF IPR Policy, *supra* note 6, at Sec. 4.A ("The [IETF] disclaims any responsibility for identifying the existence of or for evaluating the applicability of any IPR, disclosed or otherwise, to any IETF technology, specification, or standard, and will take no position on the validity or scope of any such IPR.")

4 For an in-depth discussion of the meaning of "essentiality" in the standardization context, see Jorge L. Contreras, *Essentiality and Standards-Essential Patents*, 1 *in* CAMBRIDGE HANDBOOK OF TECHNICAL STANDARDIZATION LAW: COMPETITION, ANTITRUST, AND PATENTS 209–230 (Jorge L. Contreras ed., 2017).

compliance with the Standard. This clause excludes from the definition of "Essential Claims" any Claims that are infringed only by implementations of Optional Portions or Informative Portions of the Standard. Requiring disclosure and/or licensing of Claims that cover only Optional Portions or Informative Portions of a Standard can give rise to antitrust issues and should be undertaken only after careful legal analysis. See *ABA Handbook on the Antitrust Aspects of Standards Setting.*

1. Some SDOs require that Essential Patent Claims are those that read on a Mandatory Portion of a Standard, but they do not require compliance with "all" Mandatory Portions of the Standard. These SDOs permit "sub-setting," so that, for example, a Licensing Commitment may apply as long as all of the Mandatory Portions that apply to that implementation are being implemented. This can be important, for example, if certain Implementers are creating implementations of a portion of a Standard so that their products can be incorporated into a more complete implementation by another company. See further discussion under "***Mandatory Portions.***"

Exclusions. Below are certain exclusions from the definition of "Essential Claims" that SDOs may wish to consider including in their policies:

- *Claims in the same patent that are not Necessarily Infringed.* A patent usually contains multiple claims. Even if one claim in a patent meets the definitions of being an Essential Claim, the other claims in that patent that do not meet that definition are specifically excluded from being Essential Claims.
- *"Out of scope" implementations.* SDOs and Working Groups may specify a Scope that defines the areas of

technology and permissible uses for the Standard. If a Claim defines an implementation that is outside of the Scope, then the Claim is not an Essential Claim if this exclusion is included. See definition of "Scope."

- *Enabling technologies.* In many cases, Implementers may require licenses under patents covering aspects of products described in a Standard even when those aspects are not themselves covered by the Standard. These are termed "enabling technologies." Where Essential Claims relate only to the matters specifically described in the Standard, Claims covering "enabling technologies" may be considered "Essential Claims"; however, SDOs should consider the impact of excluding such technologies through such a provision if such technologies are required to implement the Standard. For example, a Standard may cover only a narrowly defined mechanical dimension on an integrated circuit. In this example, the Implementer could argue that the Standard requires the Patent Holder to license all semiconductor manufacturing technology so as to comply with the mechanical dimension of the integrated circuit described in the Standard. To avoid this argument, this clause specifically excludes from "Essential Claims" any "enabling technologies." The nature of "enabling technologies" differs greatly depending on the nature of the Standard. Thus, it is difficult to provide comprehensive examples of the types of technologies that may be generally considered to be enabling in any given case.

*"**Final Standard**" means any Standard Document that has been [approved/published] by an SDO in accordance with [the SDO's approval process as described in [reference to SDO approval process]].*

A Final Standard is the standard that is generally published by the SDO and adopted within the industry. Contrast to "***Draft Standard.***"

> "***Implementer***" *means any person or entity [2] who makes, uses, sells, distributes, imports, or otherwise disposes of any product, or practices any method, that embodies all [or any portion of] a Standard. [Optional: For the avoidance of doubt, "Implementer" is not limited to any particular position in a supply chain.[1]]*

Implementers are entities that manufacture, sell, use, or otherwise deal in products that incorporate one or more of the SDO's standards. This definition is important, as it often describes the entities that are entitled to receive licenses under Essential Claims (see Section III).

1. *Supply chain.* The Optional language clarifies that any entity that incorporates or uses a Standard in a product or service, regardless of that person's or entity's position in a given supply chain, should be considered an implementer (and thus entitled to receive a license under Essential Claims). However, the absence of this language does not imply that Patent Holders have the right to discriminate based on an entity's position in a given supply chain.
2. *Membership.* The Policy may or may not require that Implementers be Participants in the SDO. Some consortia and smaller SDOs require that Patent Holders grant licenses only to other SDO Participants, and not to the public at large. Limiting these benefits to SDO Participants may give rise to heightened legal risks under antitrust and competition laws.

"Individual Participant" *means an individual person who is a Participant in an SDO.*

Contrast with "Participating Organization."

"Informative Portion"

See definition of ***"Mandatory Portion."***

"Informative Reference"

Not Needed for Use: A specification or other document to which reference is made in the Standard that assists the user with regard to a particular subject area but is not indispensable for the implementation of the Standard. [1]

Not Needed for Conformance: The whole or parts of a document where the referenced document has been used as supplementary information in the preparation of the Standard or to assist in the understanding or use of the Standard and to which conformance is not necessary. [2]

1. References to informational materials can be useful for background or for illustrative purposes. Unlike Normative References, Informative References are not an indispensable part of the standard and need not be implemented for the standard to be used.
2. Some SDOs define references as informative so long as an implementation of the reference is not required to claim conformance. While not necessary for conformance, such references could be indispensable for the use of the standard.

> *"**Knowledge**" means the actual, personal awareness by an individual of information relating to a particular matter, [as well as information relating to such matter that such individual reasonably should have known by virtue of his or her position] [1] [without any duty to conduct patent searches]. [2]*
>
> *[Knowledge shall not be deemed to include knowledge held by other personnel of the relevant Individual Participant's Sponsor, provided that such Sponsor will not deliberately withhold relevant information from Individual Participants in the SDO's activities for the purpose of avoiding disclosure or licensing under this Policy.] [3]*

It is important to define "knowledge" in the context of an SDO patent policy, as many SDOs limit the obligation to disclose Essential Claims to the Knowledge of a Participant. This criterion is almost always applied to the Individual Participants who participate in activities of the SDO, rather than institutionally to the Participating Organization that employs or sponsors the Individual Participant.[5]

1. One extension of the personal knowledge of the SDO Participants is knowledge that such Participant "reasonably should have known" by virtue of his or her position. This criterion would prevent a Participating Organization from deliberately insulating its personnel from patent

[5] The limitation to individual knowledge has become common after the Federal Trade Commission's action against Dell Computer, which found that Dell had committed an unfair method of competition in violation of the FTC Act by failing to disclose a patent that was not within the personal knowledge of Dell's representative to the relevant SDO, but likely within the knowledge of others at the company, including its legal department. *See In re.* Dell Computer Corp., 121 F.T.C. 616 (1996).

information for purposes of thwarting the Knowledge requirement of the Policy. It should also be pointed out, however, that such "constructive knowledge" criteria could introduce a significant element of uncertainty into the Knowledge determination. Note the ANSI patent policy does not address the issue of Knowledge. ANSI has stated in testimony that Knowledge will not be imputed to Individual Participants in the development of American National Standards.

2. Given that many organizations that participate in standards development have large patent portfolios, SDOs may wish to state that Participants are not required to conduct "patent searches" in order to discover Essential Claims. Patent searches, for this purpose, would include both reviews of internal patent department records as well as searches of public patent databases. It should be noted that the policies of many SDOs (including, for example, the Telecommunications Industry Association [TIA], the European Telecommunications Standards Institute [ETSI], and the International Telecommunications Union [ITU]) explicitly state that patent searches are not required.[6]
3. This clause limits Knowledge to that information known by Individual Participants, and it also prevents Sponsors from deliberately insulating its personnel from patent information for purposes of thwarting the Knowledge requirement of the Policy.

---

6 *See*, e.g., ETSI, Rules of Procedure, Annex 6 (IPR Policy), Section 4.1 (Sep. 3, 2020) [hereinafter ETSI Policy] ("The obligations pursuant to Clause 4.1 above do however not imply any obligation on MEMBERS to conduct IPR searches"); IEEE-SA Standards Board Bylaws, Sec. 6.2 (Aug. 2020) [hereinafter IEEE Policy] ("Nothing in this policy shall be interpreted as giving rise to a duty to conduct a patent search.")

> *"**Licensing Call**" means a [written] request from an SDO to one or more Participants to submit a Licensing Statement.*

It should be noted that a Licensing Call is distinguished from a "call for patent disclosures." See Section III.B.2[6] and B.3[5]. For additional commentary, see Section IV.C.2.c.

> *"**Licensing Commitment**" means a Participant's commitment to grant a license under Essential Claims on terms specified in Section IV.A.*

A Licensing Commitment contains a description of the terms (such as "reasonable and nondiscriminatory" license terms) that a Participant agrees to offer to all Implementers of a Standard under the Participant's Essential Claims. As described in Section IV, a Licensing Commitment may arise as a condition of participation in an SDO or may be voluntarily undertaken by a Participant when making a Licensing Statement. The Licensing Commitment is not an actual license, but an agreement to make a license available upon request. A willingness to license can be communicated as a Licensing Commitment in a Licensing Statement (see definition of "***Licensing Statement***" below).

> *"**Licensing Statement**" means a written statement submitted by a Participant to an SDO [in the form required by this Policy] [1] that describes the terms, if any, under which such Participant [hereby does] [2] [commits to] [is willing to][is prepared to] [3] license Essential Claims [listed or identified in __].*

As described in Section IV.C, some SDOs may require that a Participant disclose its position regarding licensing of Essential Claims at specified times during the standards-development process.

1. This phrase should be included if a specified form of Licensing Statement is required. See Section IV.C.3 below.
2. A policy that provides that a party "hereby does" grant a license would obviate the need for subsequent licensing negotiations and so could facilitate more immediate adoption of the standard. A policy that provides for a commitment to license binds that licenses will be granted, but leaves the details and terms of such licenses for subsequent negotiations consistent with the terms (such as RAND) chosen by the SDO.
3. In this context, there is no meaningful difference between a party that "commits to," "is willing to," or "is prepared to" grant licenses. In all such circumstances, the commitment to license Essential Claims on terms (such as RAND) specified in the Licensing Statement is likely to have legal force, and Implementers will have greater certainty regarding the terms or nature of the terms that will be offered when they implement Standards covered by the Participant's Essential Claims. This commitment is a "Licensing Commitment."

Other terms used by SDOs for Licensing Statements include "Letter of Assurance," "Licensing Declaration," and "Patent Holder Statement."

*A "**Mandatory Portion**" of a Standards Document typically conveys criteria that must always be fulfilled in order to claim full conformance to the Standard.*

*An "**Optional Portion**" of a Standards Document typically contains those Portions or criteria of a Standard that may, but are not required to, be selected in an implementation of the Standard.*

*An "**Informative Portion**" typically refers to language in a Standards Document that is only informative or* *permissive, such as the background leading to the need for the Standard, or other references in the area that may be of interest to the reader. Informative Portions are not intended to be implemented in the Standard.*

*An "**Alternative Portion**" typically exists when there is more than one way to satisfy a Mandatory Portion or an Optional Portion.*

These terms are being discussed in the same section in order to clarify how they differ and possibly overlap. Some or all of these terms may be used to define the Essential Claims that may be subject to the Policy as well as the portions of the Standard that may be subject to a Licensing Commitment.

"Mandatory Portions" also can be called "normative," "required," etc. Sometimes these portions are labeled as such in the standard. Sometimes they are identified through obligatory terms such as "shall" or "must." In some SDOs, the term "normative" is used to designate any portion of a standard that is implementable, whether mandatory, alternative, or optional.

"Optional Portions" of a Standard are, as the term implies, optional, and are not required in order to claim conformance to the Standard. Typically, "Optional Portions" contain mandatory language such as "shall" or "must" because they delineate requirements that must be met if an Implementer voluntarily chooses to implement the Optional Portion. Sometimes the term "Optional" is used by an SDO to refer to what is referred to herein as "Informative Portions," and *vice versa*, so it is important to ascertain the nature of the text being included under the chosen label. Sometimes Optional Portions and/or Informative Portions are labeled as such in the Standard. Some SDOs use the term Informative Portion only to refer to text that contains only informational or permissive language such as "should" or "may" or other descriptive material.

As noted above, even though its implementation is not required for full conformance to the standard, an Optional Portion may contain obligatory language (such as "shall" or "must"). Under these circumstances, if an Implementer does choose to implement the Optional Portion, then it must do so in accordance with these mandatory requirements. As noted *infra*, an SDO's Policy may apply only to Mandatory Portions of a Standard. Some SDOs may choose to have their policies apply explicitly to Optional Portions that contain mandatory language. In *Intel v. Via*,[7] the court found some "options" of a standard to be "required." Thus, if the Standard has a core to which options may be attached, and if attached the Claim is needed for the option, the SDO should specify whether such Claims are Essential Claims subject to obligations of disclosure and/or licensing under the SDO's rules.

Mandatory Portions and/or Optional Portions may or may not include "Alternative Portions," where an implementer must select from one of two or more alternative approaches in order to claim full conformance to the Standard. While each Alternative Portion may itself be "optional" because it does not have to be selected, an SDO may or may not seek to ensure that any Essential Patent Claims that read on any of these Alternative Portions are subject to the SDO's Policy to prevent all such Alternative Portions from arguably being blocked in this regard. Accordingly, an SDO may treat Alternative Portions in the same way it treats Mandatory Portions and/or Optional Portions that include obligatory language. Some SDOs may define "Mandatory Portions" or "Normative Portions" to apply to all of these types of Portions in order to clarify what its Policy applies to.

It should be noted that competition issues must be considered in this regard. While an SDO seeking licensing commitments *vis-à-vis* complementary or blocking patents generally

---

[7] 174 F. Supp. 2d 1038 (N.D. Cal 2001).

avoids antitrust scrutiny, the pro-competitive perspective is not so clear for alternatives or substitute technologies.

Similar competition concerns can arise when an SDO requires a Patent Holder to offer license terms covering Optional Portions as part of a package including Essential Claims, or when the Patent Holder requires that an Implementer license Claims covering Optional Portions as part of a package including Essential Claims covering Mandatory Portions.

> *A Claim is "**Necessarily Infringed**" when there is no [commercially/technically feasible/reasonable] [1] noninfringing alternative for implementing a portion of a Standard, [or when all alternative approaches are covered by such Claim and other Claims [Controlled by the same Participant or in the same patent]].*

This definition is typically used within the definition of "***Essential Claim***" to limit such Claims to those that are unavoidably infringed by all implementations of a standard.

1. The SDO must determine whether there must be absolutely *no* way to implement the Standard without infringing the Claim, or whether qualifications (such as the commercial or technical feasibility or reasonableness) may apply. The unmodified "no noninfringing alternative" language results in a more limited definition of Essential Claim, while adding a "commercially feasible" qualification, for example, makes more Claims into Essential Claims. However, the boundaries of what is "commercially feasible" may be less clear.

The difference between the terms "technically" and "commercially" can be illustrated by the example of a standard for an "alarm." Suppose that initially the only alarm that complies with the standard is a bell that costs $1.00. A Claim that covers the bell will be an Essential Claim, irrespective of whether the definition states that there must be no "technically" reasonable noninfringing alternatives or no "commercially" reasonable noninfringing alternatives. However, the situation changes when the Patent Holder or a third party develops a buzzer that also complies with the alarm standard. The buzzer costs $0.10, making the bell implementation cost-prohibitive in the commercial market. If Essential Claims are defined as those for which there is no "commercially" reasonable noninfringing alternative, the Claim on the buzzer becomes an Essential Claim, because it would not be commercially feasible to use a bell costing 10 times the cost of the buzzer. If the Policy, however, required that there be no "technically feasible" alternative in order for a Claim to be an Essential Claim, then neither the bell nor the buzzer Claims would be Essential Claims, because there would be a technical alternative for each.

An SDO policy may require the judgment regarding the "technical" or "commercial" reasonableness to be determined at a specific time, e.g., when the standard is approved or published, so that an Essential Claim cannot change its characterization. Consideration should be given to competition issues before adoption of a policy that omits a specific reference time, especially when assessing whether or not there is any "commercially reasonable" noninfringing alternative.

Under the traditional definition of "Necessarily Infringed," if there are only two claimed technical alternatives that may be implemented to achieve compliance, neither is an Essential Claim. An SDO may consider whether to include such alternative claims as Essential Claims at least in certain cases—such as when the two claims are in the same patent or in patents Controlled by the same Participant. For example, if a specification requires an alarm and a Participant has two claims in a patent on the only two technically feasible alarms, a bell and a buzzer, where one of the two claims must be infringed to implement the specification, the SDO might consider whether such Claims should be Essential Claims.

*"**Normative Portion**"*

See definition of "***Mandatory Portion***."

*"**Normative Reference**"*

Needed for Use: A specification or other document to which reference is made in the Standard in such a way as to make it indispensable for the application of the Standard. [1]

Needed for Conformance: The whole or parts of a document to which it is necessary to conform in order to claim conformance with the Standard containing the reference. [2]

The determination of whether a reference is "Normative" or "Informative" may affect what Licensing Commitments are available to Implementers, as discussed in Section V. As a result, SDOs should carefully define the term to satisfy both the SDO's and implementers' expectations regarding such Licensing Commitments. Patent Holders can be asked to license their Essential Claims covering Normative References to Implementers, as they are asked to license Essential Claims covering Normative Portions of the standard. However, while many SDO policies set forth express rules governing patent licensing and disclosure rules for Essential Claims that cover Normative Portions, not all SDOs require licensing or have disclosure policies directed to Normative References. Policies that do address Normative References often have no licensing or disclosure policies for Informative References.

Many SDOs expressly exclude Normative References from the scope of their Policy, in part because the referenced material may have been developed under a different patent policy (see discussion *infra* at V.1). A concern in excluding technology or standards that are referenced is that the standard may be unimplementable or impaired without such necessary technologies available.

1. When a Standard references another document, as opposed to copying the contents of the document into the Standard, the contents nonetheless may be an important part of the Standard. Some SDOs define such references as "normative" when the standard cannot be implemented or practiced without the use of the referenced document. In some SDOs, the referenced document may be virtually any written material but most often is a specification or Standard developed by another SDO, while in others, such as the International organization for Standardization and the International Electrotechnical Commission (ISO/IEC), the criteria for documents that may be used as Normative References are prescribed in detail (see Section 6.2.2 of 2004 ISO/IEC Directives, Part 2).
2. Some SDOs prefer to more narrowly define normative references as those that are required for conformance. For example, a standard for making emergency calls may not be usable without certain telecommunications protocols. However, conformance may be based solely on a device being able to generate a message for transmission as defined by the standard.

"*Optional Portion*"

See definition of "Mandatory Portion."

*"**Participant**" means an individual or organization that Participates in the Standards-related activity of the SDO.*

Depending on the SDO, "Participants" may be either individuals or organizations that designate individual personnel to participate in SDO activities. In either case, "Participant" is the general term used to describe a person or entity that Participates in the Standards-related work of an SDO. If "Participant" is used to designate an entity, the SDO may decide to clarify that certain obligations (such as a disclosure obligation) are triggered only by the knowledge or conduct of that entity's "Individual Participant." While a Participant may also be an Implementer, these terms are not synonymous, as there may be Participants who do not implement a Standard, and there may be Implementers of a Standard who do not participate in its development. In SDOs where membership is individual based, the SDO may seek or expect a level of obligation from the individual's Sponsor.

*"**Participate**" means active participation in an activity of an SDO, whether by making a Contribution or otherwise acting in a manner intended to influence the outcome of a discussion relating to any Standards Document [1]. Without limiting the generality of the foregoing, an Organizational Participant shall be deemed to Participate in a Working Group if any of its employees [are members/have attended ___ or more meetings of the Working Group] [during any 12-month period][1], made any Contribution to the Working Group [during the most recent 12-month period], and an individual Participant shall be deemed to Participate in a Working Group if he or she [is a member thereof/has attended ___ or more meetings] [during the most recent 12-month period],*

made any Contribution to the Working Group [during the most recent 12-month period].

SDOs with different procedures may wish to tailor their definitions of what it means to "Participate" in the activities of the SDO.

1. In some cases, SDOs may wish to avoid imposing disclosure and licensing obligations on passive observers of SDO activities (sometimes referred to as "lurkers"), thus requiring that "Participation" include active participation through the submission of Contributions or other affirmative actions intended to influence the standardization process.
2. The 12-month period in this clause is intended to provide a time period that is significant, but not unduly so. An SDO may elect to choose a time period that is longer or shorter, depending on standards development cycles and other relevant factors in its particular industry. Alternately, an SDO may elect not to use any specified time period.

*"**Participation Agreement**" means a document describing or referring to the Policy that an individual or organization must agree to in order to be a member of, or Participate in, the standards development activity of the SDO.*

This definition is relevant when an SDO has a membership (or Working Group membership) that is defined by the act of agreeing to a Participation Agreement. Such an agreement is also referred to sometimes as a "Membership Agreement." (See Section II.A regarding SDOs with no Participation Agreement.)

> *"**Participating Organization**" means a company, corporation, agency, institution, or other entity other than an individual person that is a Participant in the SDO or that sponsors the participation of one or more Individual Participants.*

In SDOs that consider Participants to be organizations, the actions of individuals representing or sponsored by such organizations are likely to be treated as actions of the organizational Participant. Accordingly, an organization should be careful to select appropriate personnel to participate in SDO activities.

> *"**Patent Disclosure**" means a [written] [1] statement submitted by a Participant to an SDO [in the form required by this Policy] [2] that describes specific Essential Claims relating to a particular Standards Document.*

1. While most SDOs require that Patent Disclosures be made in written form (which may include electronic e-mail, web posting, or other electronic forms of communication), some SDOs also permit Patent Disclosures to be made orally at certain SDO meetings, as described in Section III, Option 3 below.
2. The use of a specific, required form for Patent Disclosures is discussed in Section III.C below.

> *"**Patent Holder**" means, with respect to a particular Claim, a person or entity that Controls a Patent including such Claim.*

It should be noted that a Patent Holder may or may not be a Participant in the SDO.

> ***"Policy"*** *means this [Intellectual Property Rights/Patent] Policy.*

SDOs may have a complete IPR policy that includes a patent policy or a stand-alone patent policy.

> ***"RAND"*** *means "reasonable and nondiscriminatory" license terms and conditions.*

Many Licensing Commitments require that the Patent Holder be willing to grant or agree to offer licenses that contain RAND terms and conditions. (Some SDOs may refer to RAND "terms," which is generally understood to mean "terms and conditions.") There is not a precise legal definition of RAND. It is generally understood, however, that RAND licenses may be royalty-bearing or may include other reasonable fees. Additionally, at least one SDO (the Institute for Electrical and Electronic Engineers, IEEE) has defined "reasonable rate" to include the consideration of (1) the value contributed "to the value of the relevant functionality of the smallest saleable Compliant Implementation that practices the Essential Patent Claim," (2) the value contributed "in light of the value contributed by all Essential Patent Claims for the same IEEE Standard practice in that [smallest saleable] Compliant Implementation," and (3) "Existing licenses" that "were not obtained under the explicit or implicit threat of" an injunction and "otherwise sufficiently comparable" circumstances and resulting licenses.

RAND licenses may include other terms and conditions in addition to royalty and fee terms. These, too, must be reasonable. However, an SDO may wish to permit or prohibit specific terms and conditions in RAND licenses as described in detail in Section IV.A.

"Nondiscriminatory" generally signifies that the licensor must not refuse to license different parties on materially similar terms. There are debates as to the precise contours of the nondiscrimination obligation; one factor that may be considered in assessing the presence or absence of discrimination is the similarity, or lack thereof, between the relevant market participants and their respective businesses. In any event, it is widely recognized that standard-essential patent (SEP) licensing terms should not be used to pick-and-choose winners and losers amongst market participants. Typically, the "nondiscriminatory" requirement is satisfied if a Patent Holder is willing to offer one version of the license to any and all Implementers, regardless of where the Implementer is situated in a given supply chain (and the royalty must also otherwise be reasonable). However, given that different Implementers may want different license scopes or have different consideration to offer in return, "nondiscriminatory" does not mean that the terms of all licenses offered or granted must be identical.[8]

As with any licensing negotiation, licensors and licensees do not always agree on the reasonableness of the terms offered or requested. A RAND commitment means that the Patent Holder must grant or offer a license under its Essential Claims on terms and conditions that are reasonable and nondiscriminatory.

Other common variants of RAND include:

"Fair, Reasonable and Nondiscriminatory" (FRAND). This formulation is used primarily in Europe. Despite the addition of the word "fair," there is widespread consensus that there is no discernable legal distinction between FRAND and

---

[8] For an in-depth discussion of the nondiscrimination prong of FRAND commitments, *see* Jorge L. Contreras & Anne Layne-Farrar, *Non-Discrimination and FRAND Commitments, in* CAMBRIDGE HANDBOOK OF TECHNICAL STANDARDIZATION LAW: COMPETITION, ANTITRUST, AND PATENTS 186 (2017).

RAND requirements. In addition, at the Global Standards Collaboration, it was agreed that the terms FRAND and RAND reflected the same concept across the continents and the difference in terminology was more linguistic than substantive. This agreement was reflected in its Resolution GSC11/19 entitled "Intellectual Property Rights Policies."

"Reasonable terms and conditions that are demonstrably free of unfair discrimination": A similar version of this formulation (that simply omitted the words "and conditions") was used by ANSI at least as early as 1974. It remains in the current ANSI *Essential Requirements*. Because this language is somewhat more cumbersome than RAND, and because of the additional uncertainty introduced by the terms "demonstrably" and "unfair," some ANSI-accredited SDOs and non-ANSI-accredited SDOs have moved away from this formulation to RAND.

> *"**RANDz**" means "reasonable and nondiscriminatory" license terms [that do not include [monetary compensation/royalties]].*

Licenses granted on a RANDz basis (where "z" signifies "zero") are subject to a RAND requirement (see above) and are also intended to exclude royalties (for example, payments based on product sales) and, in some cases, other monetary consideration (such as up-front license fees) for the license grant.

Some SDOs that have adopted RANDz licensing policies may wish to exclude all monetary compensation, while others may wish to exclude only royalties. For clarity, it is recommended that an SDO specify whether RANDz signifies an exclusion of all compensation or an exclusion only of royalties.

Likewise, a number of SDOs have implemented so-called "Royalty-Free" Licensing Commitments, such as the World

Wide Web Consortium (W3C0), Bluetooth SIG, and USB Promoters Forum. The current ANSI patent policy provides RANDz as an alternative to RAND and uses the term "without compensation." See the definition of "***RAND***" for further discussion of RAND terms and conditions.

> *"**Scope**" means [describe the technical scope of the standards activity].*

The "Scope" definition may be used to limit Essential Claims subject to the Policy or may work in tandem with the Essential Claim definition to narrow the Licensing Commitment. "Scope" typically defines the technological boundaries (for example the protocols, electrical signaling characteristics, connection, methods, tools, test scripts, register models, application program interfaces, physical dimensions and characteristics, data structures, mechanical requirements, and firmware descriptors, device, and driver architectures) to the extent disclosed with particularity in the Final Standard where the sole purpose of such disclosure is to enable products incorporating the Final Standard to interoperate, interconnect, or communicate as defined in the Final Standard. The "Scope" definition may also exclude "enabling technologies" and specific technologies, such as microprocessors or busses.

> *"**Sponsor**" means the organization, if any, that employs or has otherwise sponsored an Individual Participant's participation in the activities of the SDO. For purposes of this Policy, the activities of such a sponsored Individual Participant in relation to the SDO are deemed to constitute actions of the Sponsor.*

In some SDOs, Participation is deemed to be solely by Individual Participants, and such individuals are said to attend

SDO meetings and deliberations in their individual capacities. Nevertheless, it is widely recognized that many Individual Participants in today's technical standards activities are employed by companies with a corporate interest in the standards under development, and that it would be naïve to proceed as though such companies had no influence over the actions of their employees. Accordingly, this definition seeks to link the actions of Individual Participants with their Sponsors. As a result, companies who wish their employees to participate in standards development activities should carefully instruct such employees to comply with the requirements of this Policy.

This is not to say that every Individual Participant must have an associated "Sponsor." Some individuals participate in standards-setting activities out of personal or academic interest. In particular, members of the academic community, even though employed by academic or research institutions, may do so in their individual capacities, and not "on behalf of" their institution. Indicators of whether an individual's involvement in SDO activities has been sponsored by a company or institution include: who pays for the individual's attendance at SDO meetings, whether the individual uses personal or company-supplied equipment to participate in SDO activities, whether the individual participates in SDO activities during business hours or in his or her spare time, whether the individual works with (or takes instruction from) other employees of the same company on matters relating to the SDO, whether the individual reports his or her activities regarding the SDO to the company, and whether the company or institution may receive any direct or indirect benefit from the outcome of the standards development process.

*"**Standard**" means any Draft Standard or Final Standard.*

This definition is intended to cover any deliverable produced within the context of the SDO that establishes engineering and technical requirements for processes, procedures, practices, and methods. Standards may also be established for selection, application, and design criteria for material. There are various terms that SDOs employ to reference their respective work products. Terms typically employed, in addition to "Standard," include "specification" and "recommendation." For purposes of this document, the term "Standard" will be used to signify all of these.

> *"**Standards Document**" means any written document within the standards development process of the SDO, including any interim or final version of a document setting forth all or any part of a Standard.*

Examples of such documents may include technical contributions, output of technical Working Group or committee meetings, preballot versions, or ballot versions of a Standard. Standards Documents are generally understood not to include external third-party documents that may be circulated within an SDO for informational or other purposes, including white papers, documentation for existing products, and the like.

> *"**Working Group**" or "WG" means a designated subgroup of Participants that is responsible for the development of one or more particular Standards within an SDO.*

Each SDO has its own terminology to describe the hierarchy or structure of its standards-development program. In addition to Working Group, SDOs may use terms such as Technical Committee, Technical Working Group, Subcommittee, Drafting Group, Ad Hoc Group, etc. For purposes of this Policy, the term "Working Group" will be used to indicate the group of Participants that actively develop a particular Standard.

SECTION II

General Terms

The clauses in this Section describe the manner in which this Policy becomes binding on Participants.

A. EFFECT OF POLICY

[Option 1: SDOs with a Participation Agreement]

This policy is made a part of and incorporated into each Participation Agreement.

[Option 2: SDOs with No Participation Agreement]

Any person who participates in any organized activity of SDO, including subscribing to any mailing list, participating in any online discussion, attending any meeting or teleconference, providing input to any Standards Document, or otherwise participating, shall be bound by this Policy.

Many SDOs require Participating Organizations or Individual Participants to sign a Participation Agreement by which they and their personnel are bound. This clause refers to the Participation Agreement but does not assume that the Policy forms a part of the Participation Agreement. This Policy may be a stand-alone SDO policy or it may be included in the Participation Agreement. If the Policy is embedded into individual Participation Agreements, then this clause is not necessary.

If a Participation Agreement is used, the SDO should consider appropriate measures to have a person with sufficient legal authority execute the Participation Agreement and to bind the relevant Participating Organization, if any.

Some SDOs require no written Participation Agreement and seek to bind individuals and Participating Organizations to this Policy through their conduct. That is, if the Policy is clearly posted and clearly states that participation in SDO activities constitutes assent to the Policy, then it would be difficult for a Participant to argue that the Policy did not apply to its participation. This approach has often been taken by long-standing SDOs with a broad membership base that engage in a diverse range of standardization activities (often referred to as "traditional" SDOs).

B. NONCOMPLIANCE

Policy violations can occur as a result of a Participant's failure to submit Patent Disclosures or Licensing Statements when and if required, submission of nonconforming Patent Disclosures or Licensing Statements that are not corrected as provided in Section V.B (assuming a required form of submission exists), or the intentional/reckless submission of false information in a Patent Disclosure or Licensing Statement. Each of these violations may impair the standards development process and SDOs may wish to consider specifying specific consequences of such violations. The consequences listed in this Section II.B are merely examples, and every SDO should consider carefully the potential impact of Policy violations on its particular activities as well as any adverse impact of the proposed remedies.

It should also be noted that allegations of violations of SDO Policies may lead to investigations and enforcement activities by competition agencies (in addition to litigation brought by private parties). The following language addresses an illustrative, non-exhaustive list of examples that SDOs may consider in the event of noncompliance:

> *In the event that a Participant materially [and intentionally] violates this Policy [and such violation is not cured within [___] days following notification of such violation from the SDO], then the SDO [shall/may] take any of the following action(s):*
>
> **I. Any Contribution submitted by the violating Participant may be rejected by the SDO, and any Standards Document published by the SDO that may be affected by such violation may, in the SDO's sole discretion, be withdrawn by the SDO.**
>
> **II. An SDO may post a warning or disclaimer on or in relation to the Standard, disclosing the alleged violation.**
>
> **III. The violating Participant's right to Participate in the SDO shall be revoked [permanently/for the next [time period]].**
>
> **IV. The violating Participant shall be required to grant a [RAND] [RANDz] license to all [Participants/Implementers] with respect to the Claims that are the subject of the violation, OR [5] the violating Participant shall be required to make a nonassertion covenant to all [Participants/Implementers] with respect to the Claims that are the subject of the violation.**

Needless to say, the issue of penalties for SDO policy violations can be a sensitive one. First, the SDO must consider whether all violations of its policy will be subject to the remedies described in this Section, or whether only intentional violations will be so treated. While unintentional violations (through neglect, simple inadvertence, or the complexity of assessing the applicability of Claims to standards) may impair the standards development process equally as much as intentional violations, many SDO Participants could be uncomfortable with facing severe remedies for unintentional violations. Penalizing Participants for unintentional violations could thus deter potential Participants from joining SDOs.

1. *Rejection of Violator's Contributions/Standards.* An SDO must be careful in exercising the right to reject a violator's Contributions in light of its potential impact on other Participants. An SDO exercising the remedy of rejecting a Contribution from a Participant that it believes has violated its Policy may expose itself and potentially its members to claims that the remedy is a group refusal to deal in violation of Section 1 of the Sherman Act, 15 U.S.C. § 1.
2. *Posting of Warning.* Typically, the disclaimer is to the effect that there might be essential patent claims that read on the standard that were more recently disclosed.
3. *Ejection from the SDO.* While ejection from the SDO may seem to be a fair response to a Participant's violation of SDO policies, an SDO should consider potential countervailing pressures not to expel such Participants. For example, the loss of key technical players may weaken the SDO's standards, expelled Participants may join or form competing SDOs, or they may become unwilling to license their patents to implementers of the expelling SDO's standards.
4. *Automatic License Grant.* This remedy requires that the violator grant either RAND or RANDz licenses under the Essential Claims in question. Such a measure, particularly in the case of a RANDz license, could act as a significant deterrent to violations of the policy, but might be viewed as draconian by Participants. The distinction, if any, between a license and a covenant not to sue is discussed in Section IV.C.1 below.

SECTION III

Patent Disclosures

One of the key elements of an SDO Policy describes when, and if, Participants are required, encouraged, or permitted to disclose Essential Claims that may have a bearing on the Standards being developed by the SDO. The Standards development and approval process is likely to be more efficient if the existence of Essential Claims, and the Licensing Commitment under which such Essential Claims may be licensed, is known as early as possible in the development process. Early disclosure affords Participants the greatest opportunity to request a license or information regarding the Patent Holder's licensing terms and to assess whether or not it is desirable to advance a standard incorporating the patented technology. Conversely, the discovery of Essential Claims that are not available for licensing during the late stages of standards development or after a standard has been approved may result in a standard that is impractical to implement and the waste of considerable effort by the Participants.

Some SDOs require the disclosure of Essential Claims by their Participants. One prominent example is the Internet Engineering Task Force (IETF), which imposes significant disclosure obligations, but does not impose a Licensing Commitment. Some SDOs limit the requirement to disclose Essential Claims to Patent Holders that are unwilling to make Licensing Commitments. And some SDOs, such as ETSI, require both disclosure and Licensing Commitments.

SDOs often require disclosure of "known" Claims (based on the Individual Participant's Knowledge) at the time of voting to accept or approve a Draft Standard as a Final Standard, or earlier. If a Patent Holder discloses an Essential Claim that it is not willing to license, the SDO may decline to accept/approve the Draft Standard as a Final Standard and may elect to send the Draft Standard back to the Working Group in an attempt to re-draft the standard to avoid the Essential Claim (commonly known as "working around" the relevant Claims). A consensus may also be sought to proceed with the standard. This could happen, for example, when Participants do not believe that the Claim asserted is an Essential Claim. Many SDOs encourage the disclosure of Essential Claims as early as possible in the development cycle of the Standard, so that technology covered by such Essential Claims but which is not available for licensing can be addressed or avoided early in the development process.

This being said, excising patented technology from a Standard may be difficult. Many companies wish to avoid exposing their technical experts to issues of taint or knowledge that could result if they reviewed another company's patents. In addition, patents are legal documents, and the scope of patent claims requires legal interpretation. Thus, once a patent is brought to a company's attention through disclosure to an SDO, counsel should determine what (if any) duty there may be to investigate. Any such investigation should be conducted by competent patent counsel. Patent counsel can also help weigh the benefits and risks of investigating or not investigating.

It may be difficult for a Patent Holder to disclose Claims that are Essential Claims with certainty early in the development of a standard because the technology may be undefined and determining essentiality is difficult. However, when a Participant believes that it has a Claim that may be essential to a current Draft Standard, bringing it to the attention of the SDO and Participants early in the process can benefit the standard and the standards development process. It should be noted that the representative to the SDO Working Group may not be trained in making the determination of essentiality. To avoid over-disclosing (by citing Claims that are inapposite) or under-disclosing (due to faulty understanding of the Claims or laws for interpreting Claims), an Individual Participant who believes that he or she is aware of a possible Essential Claim should have the issue reviewed by a skilled patent attorney and disclose if appropriate.

SDOs should be sensitive when drafting disclosure policies to the significant liability that may arise for Participants when they fail to comply with such policies. Such liability risks and other consequences of failure to comply with SDO disclosure requirements are discussed in Section III.F, below.

A. OBLIGATION TO DISCLOSE

SDOs may implement disclosure obligations of varying scope. Some have broad obligations that require all members of the SDO to disclose Essential Claims regardless of that member's degree of participation in the SDO or its Working Groups. Other SDOs link the disclosure obligation to those who submit a technical proposal (e.g., make a Contribution), participate in a Working Group or SDO committee, or even receive and review a copy of the draft Standard. Some SDOs may even send disclosure requests to specific companies believed to own or control patents relevant to the Standard, and responding to such requests may be voluntary (e.g., for companies who are not members of the SDO) or mandatory (for those who are members).

This Section III.A discusses three of the many possible disclosure scenarios:

- A Participant's disclosure of its Essential Claims covering its own Contributions to a Standard;
- A Participant's disclosure of its Essential Claims covering other elements of a Standard; and
- Disclosure of a third party's Essential Claims.

An SDO may wish to adopt different timing requirements as to these different scenarios. For example, an SDO may wish to require a Participant to disclose its Claims covering its own Contributions at the time of contribution, but only obligate the Participant to disclose its own Claims covering the Contributions of others at a later time. These different options are addressed in Section III.B.

For purposes of clarity, this Section has been prepared both from the perspective of an SDO whose membership consists of Participating Organizations and an SDO whose membership is based on individual membership/participation. However, because these two cases result in slightly different requirements, they have been addressed separately when so required.

1. Participant's Patents Covering Its Own Contributions

This first scenario addresses the situation in which an SDO Participant owns or controls Patents that cover the Participant's Contributions to a Standard. The following language addresses this scenario:

> *Each Participant [shall/is encouraged to/may] disclose to the SDO, in the manner set forth in this Policy, all [patents having] [Claims that may be/are believed to be] Essential Claims covering such Participant's Contributions, within the Knowledge of the Contributor that are Controlled by the Participant at any time during its Participation in [the SDO/the relevant WG]*

Participating Organizations and Individual Participants. If the SDO has only Individual Participants, then they are obligated/encouraged/permitted to make disclosures based on their own Contributions. If the SDO membership is open to Participating Organizations, then such Participating Organizations must/may make disclosures based on Contributions made by individuals that they sponsor. Similarly, for individual membership SDOs, an Individual Participant's Contribution is the Contribution made by that Individual Participant. For organizational membership SDOs, a Participating Organization's Contribution is a Contribution made by any person whose participation in an SDO activity is sponsored by the Participating Organization.

Patents and Essential Claims. Many disclosure obligations, such as the one above, require Participants to identify only those patents or patent applications that are likely to contain Essential Claims, as opposed to requiring identification of specific patent Claims. While disclosure of specific patent Claims provides greater detail to the SDO and other Participants, it is also a more onerous burden on the Patent Holder. For example, even when a complete analysis can be conducted by a patent attorney, there are still uncertainties that can affect the ultimate determination as to whether a Claim is an Essential Claim. As a result, SDOs should consider whether a Patent Holder must declare that it "has Essential Claims" or merely that it is "likely to have Essential Claims." Further, if an SDO requires disclosure of patent applications, or if a disclosure must be made prior to adoption of the Final Standard, then the Participant will be less certain that the Claims cover the relevant Standard. Accordingly, it may be desirable to give the Participant more flexibility in determining whether Claims are Essential Claims that must be disclosed.

Knowledge. Many SDOs limit disclosure obligations to information within the "Knowledge" of the relevant Contributor.[1]

---

[1] For example, *see* OASIS, IPR Policy, Sections 8.1 and 8.2, available at https://www.oasis-open.org/policies-guidelines/ipr (last accessed Sept. 14, 2020): "Each TC Party shall disclose to OASIS in writing the existence of all patents and/or patent applications owned or claimed by such TC Party that are actually known to the TC Member directly participating in the TC,

Note that "Contributor" refers to the Individual Participant making the Contribution. However, even though this Knowledge requirement may apply to an individual Contributor, if the Individual Participant breaches his or her obligation to disclose Essential Claims within his or her Knowledge, then the Sponsor could be considered to be in breach of the Policy as well. Note that the converse is also possible. An organization may be liable for failing to disclose an Essential Claim of which an Individual Participant did not know, so long as others within the organization knew of the Essential Claim (see *In re Dell*, 121 F.T.C. 616 (1996)).

Reasonable Efforts. Some SDOs, such as VITA and ETSI, do not limit disclosure to actual knowledge and instead employ a "reasonableness" approach in which the Participant is expected to make reasonable efforts to identify its Essential Claims for disclosure. VITA additionally states that the inquiry should be made in "good faith." The respective excerpts below from the IPR Policies of VITA and ETSI illustrate these requirements:

> ***VITA*** - *Each working group member ("WG Member") shall disclose to the working group ("WG") in writing the existence of all patents and patent applications owned, controlled, or licensed by the VITA member company ("VITA Member Company") the WG Member represents,*

---

and which such TC Member believes may contain any Essential Claims or claims that might become Essential Claims upon approval of an OASIS Standards Final Deliverable as such document then exists (collectively, "Disclosed Claims"). . . . it is understood and agreed that such TC Party(s)' TC Member(s) do not represent that they know of all potentially pertinent claims of patents and patent applications owned or claimed by the TC Party or any third parties. For the avoidance of doubt, while the disclosure obligation under Sections 8.1 and 8.2 applies directly to all TC Parties, this obligation is triggered based on the actual knowledge of the TC Party's TC Members regarding the TC Party's patents or patent applications that may contain Essential Claims."

which are known by the WG Member and which the WG Member believes contain claims that may become essential to the draft VSO specification ("Draft VSO Specification") of the WG in existence at the time, after the WG Member has made a good faith and reasonable inquiry into the patents and patent applications the VITA Member Company (or its Affiliates) owns, controls or licenses.[2]

ETSI *- Subject to Clause 4.2 below, each MEMBER shall use its reasonable endeavours, in particular during the development of a STANDARD or TECHNICAL SPECIFICATION where it participates, to inform ETSI of ESSENTIAL IPRs in a timely fashion. In particular, a MEMBER submitting a technical proposal for a STANDARD or TECHNICAL SPECIFICATION shall, on a bona fide basis, draw the attention of ETSI to any of that MEMBER's IPR which might be ESSENTIAL if that proposal is adopted.*[3]

Control. Many disclosure obligations (like the one above) deal with patents "Controlled" by a Participant. Because the Contributor can be assumed to have the greatest information about, and financial interest in, patents that it Controls, the disclosure requirements under this Clause are usually the most stringent. Such a requirement may deter a Contributor from directing a Standard toward its own patented technology without the knowledge of the other Participants. Other Patents of which a Participant may be aware may be subject to disclosure as third-party patents, as discussed below in Section III.A.3.

Timing. An SDO disclosure requirement may be linked either to Participation in the SDO generally, or in the specific Working Group or Draft Standard as to which Essential Claims

---

2 VITA, Policies and Procedures, Section 10.2.1 (Rev. 2.8, Sept. 1, 2015) [hereinafter VITA Policy].

3 ETSI Policy, *supra* note 11, Sec. 4.1.

would relate. An SDO that is concerned about the risk that a prospective Participant may intentionally transfer patents prior to joining the SDO and/or a Working Group so as to evade disclosure requirements may wish to consider additional Policy requirements to address this situation. In addition, an SDO may consider making regular requests for patent disclosures (e.g., at the beginning of Working Group meetings) so that a Participant does not wait until the last minute, after the Standard has been nearly completed, to disclose Essential Claims.

2. *Participant's Patents Covering Any Standards Document*

Some SDO disclosure policies may require disclosure of an SDO Participant's Essential Claims covering any Mandatory Portion of a Standards Document, whether the Participant actually contributed the relevant technology/information. The following sample language addresses this situation:

> *Each Participant [shall/is encouraged to/may] disclose to the SDO, in the manner set forth in this Policy all [Patents having] [Claims that may be/are believed to be] Essential Claims pertaining to any [Standard/Final Standard] [arising from a WG in which the Participant Participated] within the Knowledge of the Participant (for Individual Participants) or, in the case of Participating Organizations, any Individual Participant sponsored by such Participating Organization [that are Controlled by the Individual Participant or its Sponsor] at any time during its Participation in [the SDO/the relevant WG] [as well as during the time it was considering joining the SDO with respect to Claims transferred in contemplation of joining]*

Relationship to Contribution-Based Disclosure Provisions. It would be feasible for an SDO to omit Contribution-based disclosure provisions (Section A.1) if it includes Document-based disclosure provisions (this Section A.2), as the term Standards Document necessarily encompasses all Contributions made by a Participant. The reverse, however, is not true, as a Standards Document may include Contributions by multiple Participants, and an obligation to disclose Essential Claims covering one's own Contributions would not extend to parts of a Standards Document contributed by others. SDOs should carefully consider the desired scope of disclosures, as a requirement to disclose Essential Claims covering other parties' Contributions can become burdensome and might require detailed legal analysis in addition to technical familiarity with the technology in question.

Scope of Standards Document-Based Disclosure. The scope of a disclosure requirement may be limited to Final Standards, or it may include all Standards Documents. Each approach has pros and cons. Limiting disclosures to Final Standards will more definitively match disclosures to actual standards in the marketplace; however, this approach will result in disclosures made late in the standardization process, well after it is convenient to work around a standard covered by particular Essential Claims. In contrast, a disclosure requirement applicable to all Standards Documents (which includes Draft Standards) will elicit earlier disclosures that could trigger work-arounds of particular Essential Claims, but requires more work and attention by Participants, and may result in disclosures on Draft Standards that are not updated to reflect changes made by the time a Final Standard is adopted.

3. *Third-Party Claims*

In this scenario, the Participant is asked to disclose third-party Claims of which it has Knowledge that may read on a

Standard, to provide the SDO's Participants with the greatest visibility into potential patent issues with a Standard under development. Because this scenario deals with Claims that are not Controlled by the discloser, the requirement for disclosure may have to be more lenient than discussed above under Sections III.A and III.B with respect to Claims Controlled by the Participant itself. The following sample language addresses this scenario:

> *Each Participant [shall/is encouraged to/may] disclose to the SDO, in the manner set forth in this Policy all [patents having] [Claims that may be/are believed to be] Essential Claims that are Necessarily Infringed by any implementation of a Standard [within the Knowledge of the Participant (for Individual Participants) or, in the case of Participating Organizations, any Individual Participant sponsored by such Participating Organization] that are Controlled by a third party other than the Participant or, for individual Participants, its Sponsor unless the Participant is restricted from disclosing such Claim by contract, confidentiality obligation, court order, or other legal impediment.*

Potential for Abuse. In some cases, the disclosure of third-party Claims can be used in a manner that is abusive to the standards-development process. For example, a noncontributing Participant could assert that a Contributor or a third-party controls Essential Claims that may read on a Standard for the purpose of slowing or blocking adoption of the Standard. Some have raised the concern that a Participant may submit a Contribution to the SDO solely to "flush out" Claims of its competitors or to determine whether licenses will be available under such Claims. Such a requirement, however, can be highly informative to Working Group members if applied correctly and in good faith.

Relationship with Third-Party Patent Holder. Third-party disclosures, while potentially valuable to the standards-development process, could also have an effect on the Participant's relationship with the Patent Holder. A Participant may be reluctant to admit infringement of or interpret third-party Claims by means of such a disclosure. Thus, an SDO should be cautious about requiring disclosure of third-party Claims, as opposed to merely encouraging or permitting such disclosures. If a third party sues or threatens to sue an Implementer, the Implementer may reasonably disclose the same without making any admission concerning infringement or claim interpretation. Third parties could also constitute entities Controlling patents in which multiple Participants may each have a minority ownership interest.

Strength of Requirement. SDO policies differ in the degree to which they require the disclosure of known third-party IPR. The patent policy of the Organization for the Advancement of Structured Information Standards (OASIS) states that its members "should" disclose third-party IPR:

> *Each TC Party whose TC Members become aware of patents or patent applications owned or claimed by a third party that contain claims that might become Essential Claims upon approval of an OASIS Standards Final Deliverable should disclose them, provided that such disclosure is not prohibited by any confidentiality obligation binding upon them. It is understood that any TC Party that discloses third party patent claims to OASIS does not take a position on the essentiality or relevance of the third*

> *party claims to the OASIS Standards Final Deliverable in its then-current form.*[4]

On the other hand, VITA's IPR Policy imposes an affirmative duty to disclose third-party IPR, subject only to confidentiality restrictions:

> *Each WG Member who becomes aware of patents or patent applications owned or claimed by a third party that the WG Member believes to contain claims that may become essential to the Draft VSO Specification of the WG in existence at the time, including but not limited to any such patents that are licensed to the VITA Member Company the WG Member represents, must disclose them, provided that such disclosure is not prohibited by any confidentiality obligation binding upon the WG Member or the VITA Member Company he or she represents. Any WG Member that discloses third party patent claims does not take a position on the essentiality or relevance of the third party claims to the Draft VSO Specification.*[5]

B. TIMING OF PATENT DISCLOSURES

This section addresses when an SDO Participant must/may/should make the disclosures discussed in Section III.A. Timing of disclosures can have a significant impact on the standards-development process, so particular attention should be given to these considerations. If disclosure is made at an advanced stage in the process, for example, it may be too

---

4 OASIS IPR Policy, Section 8.2, available at https://www.oasis-open.org/policies-guidelines/ipr (last accessed Sept. 14, 2020).

5 VITA Policy, *supra* note 14.

late to revise the Standard to avoid infringement of Essential Claims, resulting in a Standard with additional licensing costs (or, worse, with technologies that are unavailable for licensing). On the other hand, it may be difficult to make reliable disclosures of Essential Claims when the Standard is immature and the essentiality of patented technologies is unclear; such early disclosures may result in a larger percentage of false positives or negatives as compared to disclosures when the Standard is closer to final. The different timing options described in this subsection reflect different SDO practices regarding disclosure.

1. *Upon Entry in SDO*

> *Each Participant shall make the Patent Disclosure specified in Section III.A.2 above with respect to any [Draft Standard/Final Standard] published by the SDO.*

This Clause requires an initial disclosure of a Participant's Claims covering any Standard if the disclosure obligation is triggered (such as due to an Individual Participant's knowledge). Such disclosures are useful to other SDO Participants, yet they also may impose a burden on a new Participant if it has to review a potentially large group of existing Standards Documents to determine whether any of them are covered by the Participant's Essential Claims.

2. *Examples of Timing of Disclosures*

Disclosure Earlier in the Standards Process. If an SDO wishes disclosure to be made as early as possible in the standards process, then it should consider options [1], [2], or [3] below. This will give Participants the most knowledge of potential Claims affecting their deliberations, but may also result in unnecessary disclosures (for example, if elements of a Standards Document are modified during the standards development process so as not to be covered by the disclosed Claims, or if claims of patent applications are narrowed during prosecution so that the issued patent no longer covers the relevant Standard).

> *A Participant [must] [is encouraged to] make the Patent Disclosures required pursuant to Section III.A.[1/2/3] above:*
>
> **I. promptly after the Participant first obtains Knowledge of the Claim(s) giving rise to the requirement for such Patent Disclosure.**
>
> **II. upon submission of such Contribution.**
>
> **III. at the start of the next SDO meeting following the time at which it first obtains Knowledge of the Claim(s) giving rise to the requirement for such Patent Disclosure.**

Disclosure Later in the Standards Process. If an SDO wishes the relevant technical discussions and deliberations to be more advanced before requiring Patent Disclosures to be made, then options [4], [5], or [6] below should be considered. In addition, if option [6] is selected, the SDO must establish a procedure for issuing "calls for disclosure" at periodic intervals, usually some fixed period of time prior to the vote on or approval of the publication of a Draft Standard or Final Standard.

> *A Participant [must] [is encouraged to] make the Patent Disclosures required pursuant to Section III.A.[1/2/3] above:*

IV. no later than __ days before the first scheduled vote on the relevant Draft Standard.

V. no later than __ days before the relevant [Draft Standard/Final Standard] is scheduled for publication.

VI. within __ days following the SDO's written "call for disclosures."

Additional Considerations. If a Participant is required to disclose its Essential Claims covering any portion of a Standards Document, rather than only the Participant's own Contributions, then the SDO may wish to offer the Participant a longer period of time in which to evaluate the Essential Claims and make the disclosure. Further, having a specific deadline for disclosure that is not linked to the time when the Participant first has Knowledge may make compliance more difficult. For example, if a Participant first becomes aware of an Essential Claim just a few days before a stated deadline, the Participant may not have sufficient time to conduct a legal review of the Essential Claims and Contribution in order to ensure that any Disclosure is reasonably accurate.

Call for Disclosures. Early in the standards development process, some SDOs may request that Participants disclose likely Essential Claims of which they have Knowledge.[6] Such

---

6 *See*, e.g., NFC Forum, IPR Policy, Section 3.4 (June 4, 2015), available at https://nfc-forum.org/wp-content/uploads/2013/11/NFC-Forum-IPR-Policy.pdf (last accessed Sept. 14, 2020) ("At the beginning of every in-person meeting and teleconference that occurs as a part of the technical process, and at any other appropriate time in the course of electronic collaboration as may be provided for under the Rules of Procedure, the following Patent Call shall be read: Please be aware that this meeting is being held under the Intellectual Property Rights Policy adopted by the Consortium. If you do not have a copy of this policy, please see me during this meeting. You may also view and download a copy of that policy from the Consortium

"patent calls" are often intended to be informational, rather than formal and binding, while also making Participants aware of their disclosure obligations. SDO representatives may then share information received from the patent calls with the SDO's legal advisors to guide development of the Standard. Later in the standards-development process, these SDOs may hold a formal patent call, the timing of which often coincides with when Patent Holders inform the SDO of whether they will license their Essential Claims on RAND terms.

C. FORMAT OF PATENT DISCLOSURES

This Section discusses several possibilities concerning the format of patent disclosures, including:

- The SDO provides a format that Participants must use when making patent disclosures;
- The SDO provides an optional format that Participants may use when making patent disclosures; and
- The SDO specifies certain patent information that Participants must disclose or permits blanket disclosures.

Each of these alternatives is discussed in turn below.

1. Disclosures Using a Required Format

Some SDOs, such as those handling frequent Disclosures or those that conduct a review and approval of each Patent Disclosure Statement, may wish to require that Disclosures be

---

website. At this time, I would ask that anyone in attendance inform me if they are personally aware of any claims under any patent applications or issued patents that would likely be infringed by an implementation of the Specification which is the subject of this meeting. You need not be the inventor under such patent or patent application in order to inform us of its existence, nor will you be held responsible for expressing a belief that turns out to be inaccurate.")

made using a uniform Disclosure Form. Such a form makes it easier for the SDO to compare Disclosures or to publish them in an automatic manner. If a Disclosure Form is required, the SDO should make it readily available, for example by posting it on a website or including it in the SDO Policy. Because a web posting is relatively easy to update, this approach is recommended over inclusion in the Policy, which may require more procedural steps to revise. Exemplary IPR Policy language is as follows:

> *All Patent Disclosures must be made using the Disclosure Form that can be found at www.sdo.org/disclosures. Each section of the Disclosure Form that is applicable must be completed in order for the Patent Disclosure to be accepted by the SDO. The SDO reserves the right to change the format and/or content of the Disclosure Form at any time by posting a revised Disclosure Form at the Web address listed above. All Patent Disclosures made more than [30 days] after the posting of a revised Disclosure Statement Form must use such revised Disclosure Form in order to be accepted by the SDO.*

The preparation of a mandatory form (or the revision of such a form) should have appropriate legal review to ensure that it is consistent with the applicable provisions of this Policy.

The SDO may find it necessary to update its Disclosure Form from time to time. If the form is revised by the SDO, the SDO should provide sufficient notice to the Participants of the revision and make the revised Disclosure Statement Form available to the Participants. However, so as not to disrupt Disclosures that were in preparation at the time of the revision, it is recommended that a reasonable "Grace Period" be allowed between the posting of the revised Disclosure Form and the requirement that the revised Disclosure Form be used for all

Disclosures. Following the expiration of this Grace Period, the SDO should no longer accept Disclosures made on superseded Disclosure Forms.

If the Disclosure Form was revised to reflect substantive changes in the SDO's Policy, however, the SDO may want to consider linking the Grace Period to the start of a new standards project (so that all Participants in a current project are subject to the same version of the Policy and Form). The SDO should weigh the benefits of treating all Participants equally against the ability to implement the new Policy without delay.

It is recommended that the SDO clearly list the version number or the revision date on all Disclosure Forms so that both the Participants and the SDO can easily distinguish which form is in effect. The preparation of a mandatory Disclosure Form (or the revision of such a form) should have appropriate legal review to ensure that it is consistent with the applicable provisions of this Policy. Considerations relating to the design of such forms are discussed in Appendix A.

2. Disclosures When No Specific Format Is Required

The SDO may wish to allow Participants to make Disclosures in whatever reasonable manner they desire, subject to their compliance with the other submission requirements (such as the proper submission address and the details required in any submission). For example:

> *Patent Disclosures must be in writing and submitted to the [address] set forth in Section [___] of this Policy and must include all information required by this Policy, but may otherwise be made in the manner selected by the Participant. If they so desire, Participants may, but are not*

required to, submit Patent Disclosures using the Disclosure Form that can be found at www.sdo.org/disclosures. Use of this Form is optional, and neither its use nor non-use will benefit or prejudice any Participant.

Patent Disclosures may be made in the manner selected by the Participant [whether written or oral], provided, however, that all Patent Disclosures must be clear and must include all information required by Section III.C.2 of this Policy.

This freedom is often desired by large Participating Organizations that belong to numerous standards organizations, and that wish to make Patent Disclosures using an in-house format.

Even if Participants are given the flexibility to make Disclosures in the manner they choose, the SDO may find it useful to make a "sample" or "template" Disclosure Form available. Such a Form can provide a useful starting point for Disclosures and may help to ensure that Participants structure their individual Disclosures in a way that presents all the information required by the Policy. However, if the Disclosure Form is not required, then the SDO should not penalize Participants who fail to use it, provided that their customized Disclosure forms supply all required information. In practice, many SDOs are silent regarding the format of Patent Disclosures.

3. *Content and Specificity of Patent Disclosures*

It is important that each Patent Disclosure include all information that the SDO deems to be relevant to an effective assessment of the disclosed Essential Claims. For example:

Each Patent Disclosure shall contain the following information:

A. *Name of Submitter. The name of the Participant and, if an individual, his or her Sponsor, as well as the name and contact information for one or more contact persons at such Sponsor (name, email address, and telephone number).*
B. *Patent Holder. If the Patent Holder is other than the Participant and/or Sponsor, then the name of the Patent Holder shall also be provided.*
C. *Patent Details. The patent/serial number [and issuance/filing date] of each patent or [published] patent application that contains Essential Claims being disclosed [and, if such patent contains both Essential Claims and other Claims, the number of each Essential Claim].*
D. *Standard Details. The specific Standards Document covered by each disclosed Essential Claim. [If a Standards Document has multiple independent portions, some of which are not covered by the disclosed Essential Claim, then the specific subsection(s) of the Standard that is covered by the disclosed Essential Claim shall also be listed.]*
E. *Licensing Statement. [A Licensing Statement in the form required by Section IV.C of this Policy in relation to the disclosed Essential Claim.]*
F. *Other Information. The Patent Disclosure may also include the following additional information: __________________________.*

Authorized Individuals for Disclosure. The SDO must consider who will be authorized to make Patent Disclosures on behalf of a Participant. That is, whether Patent Disclosures may be submitted only by an individual Participant, by corporate attorneys, or other designated representatives. In general, SDOs accept Patent Disclosures from any authorized corporate representative of the Participant, though evidence of authorization may be required in some cases.

Disclosure of Patent Numbers. Some SDOs require that patent or application numbers accompany each Patent Disclosure.[7] Listing patent numbers enables those reviewing Patent Disclosures more easily to identify Essential Claims that may affect standardization work. However, requiring numbers to be listed is more burdensome for disclosing Participants, particularly if large numbers of patents are applicable to a particular Standard, and also opens the possibility of unintentional omission of patents that may later be deemed to contain Essential Claims. SDOs that do not mandate the disclosure of patent numbers typically allow the disclosure of the patent number as optional information. Moreover, SDOs that permit "blanket" disclosure statements (see Section III.C.4 below) typically do not require disclosure of patent numbers.

Disclosure of Standards Documents. It is important that a Patent Disclosure identify the relevant Standards Document implicated by the disclosure. However, linking disclosure to specific subparts of a Standards Document may impose a burden on Patent Holders having multiple Essential Claims and

---

7 *See*, e.g., VITA Policy, *supra* note 14, Sec. 10.2.2 ("All patents or patent applications to be disclosed under Section 10.2.1 shall include the following information: (a) for issued patents and published patent applications, the patent or patent application number, the associated country and, as reasonably practicable, the relevant portions of the WG's Draft VSO Specification; and (b) in the case of unpublished patent applications, the existence of the unpublished patent applications and, as reasonably practicable, the relevant portions of the WG's Draft VSO Specification.")

is seldom required except in opt-out (see Section III.D below) or withdrawal situations where the Patent Holder is unwilling to license the Essential Claim.

Licensing Statement. Some SDOs require that a Licensing Statement accompany each Patent Disclosure (or that only a Licensing Statement, and no Patent Disclosure, be made). See Section IV.C.

4. *Blanket Patent Disclosures*

Some SDOs permit Participants to make broad, general disclosures to the effect that they Control or believe they Control, Essential Claims covering the SDO's standards. An example of such a "blanket" disclosure is the following: "Company X is actively developing products and technologies in the [name technology] area and consequently may file and obtain patents covering all or portions of standards developed by the SDO." Such a disclosure gives little useful information to the SDO or its Participants and is often permitted only if the disclosing Participant concurrently commits to license its Essential Claims on RAND or RANDz terms. In other words, the SDO may be willing to trade off the knowledge that is obtained from a specific Patent Disclosure for the certainty that the Patent Holder will grant licenses under the nondisclosed Essential Claims.

The following language discusses blanket disclosures:

> *A disclosure under this Policy will not be deemed to be adequate if it lacks the specific requirements set forth in [Section III.D.2] above. So-called "blanket disclosures" identifying Claims or patents in a general or broad manner without the specificity required above shall not be considered compliant with this Policy and shall be rejected by the SDO [unless accompanied by a Licensing*

Commitment that provides for [RAND or RANDz licensing of all Claims covered by such blanket disclosure.]

5. *Updating Patent Disclosures*

An SDO that requires or permits Patent Disclosures should also provide a mechanism for updating those Patent Disclosures to reflect changes in patent status (e.g., issuance or narrowing of Claims), as well as changes to Standards Documents. For example:

A Participant [must/is encouraged to] notify the SDO each time that:

A. Issuance. A Disclosed Claim of a patent application issues in an issued patent.
B. Limiting a Disclosed Claim. A Disclosed Claim of a patent application is [materially] limited during the course of patent prosecution.
C. Expiration or Invalidity. A Disclosed Claim of a patent/patent application has expired, been invalidated, or been abandoned for any reason, whether in whole or in part.
D. Revisions to Standard. A Standard is amended in such a way that it is, or is no longer, covered by a Disclosed Claim.

"Materially" suggests that the amendment to the Claim may affect the vitality of the earlier disclosure. For example, if the Claim is amended so that it no longer is/may be an Essential Claim, that fact should be disclosed to the SDO.

The life of a patent can end on a fixed date, generally 20 years after its effective filing date at the patent office. However, a patent's life can end earlier if maintenance fees are not paid, or if the patent is found by a competent government authority to be invalid or unenforceable. A Patent Holder can also terminate or shorten rights in a patent (or claims of a patent) by filing certain documentation at the patent office.

D. DISCLOSURE EXCLUSIONS, EXEMPTIONS, AND OPT-OUT

Patent Disclosures are intended to provide the SDO and its Participants with information about Essential Claims that may affect standards-development activities. Many SDOs believe that obtaining this information as early in the standards-development process as possible is beneficial to the process. Early disclosure of such Essential Claims enables Implementers to plan and assess risk, makes SDOs aware of potential Essential Claims, and enables Participants to consider design-arounds to avoid such Essential Claims.

In some SDOs, however, Patent Holders have a Licensing Commitment with respect to Essential Claims that they disclose. Some Patent Holders may not be willing to make a Licensing Commitment, especially early in a standard's development, without knowing what patents are finally implicated, what direction the standard may take, and what third-party patents may also be required to practice the standard. Moreover, Patent Holders may be reluctant to participate in an SDO if they are required to disclose (and possibly incur Licensing Commitments with respect to) Essential Claims covering Standards that they did not actively help to develop.

If key Patent Holders remain outside the SDO and its standards-development process, negative effects can result—such as vital technologies not being contributed and/or Patent Holders not being subject to the SDO's policies. Accordingly, some SDOs allow Participants to exclude (or reduce the level of Licensing Commitment for) certain Essential Claims disclosed by them. In these cases, the SDO seeks a balance between the benefits of knowing about Essential Claims early and avoiding disincentives to participation by Patent Holders and other possible negative effects (such as overbroad disclosures, delays in the process, etc.).

This Section III.D discusses three possibilities in which such exclusions can be implemented.

1. *Opt-Out for Non-Involvement*

SDO policies that require Patent Disclosures sometimes permit Participants to "opt out" of this requirement. Such exclusions, if permitted by the Policy, are generally allowed during a period in which the Participant is requested to review a Draft Standard, as demonstrated by the sample language below:

> *If a Participant is requested to review a Draft Standard during the Review Period, and if the Participant did not Participate in the Working Group that developed the Draft Standard, the Participant may "opt out" of the [requirement/request] to disclose Essential Claims under Section III.A.2 [1] by sending written notice of its intent to opt out to the SDO before the end of the Review Period.*

SDOs may undertake multiple standards development projects where some Participants Participate in only a limited number of Working Groups. A Patent Holder that Participates in a single project/Working Group may not practically be able to review every Draft Standard developed at the SDO. SDOs can respond to that concern by limiting the disclosure requirement to the Knowledge of the Patent Holder's participating employees as discussed above.

But because identifying employees that are participating and assessing their Knowledge is sometimes uncertain and not well-defined, some policies respond to the Patent Holders' concerns by providing a period in which the Patent Holder may "opt out" of the disclosure requirement if it had no involvement in the development of the relevant Draft Standard.

Note that this exclusion is relevant only when the SDO requires Patent Disclosures relative to a broad range of Draft Standards, such as described in Section III.A.2 above. A Participant may not be permitted to opt out of its obligation to make Patent Disclosures with respect to its own Contributions, as required under Section III.A.1.

2. *Exemption from Disclosure If Licensing Commitment Is Made*

Disclosure "exemptions" may be allowed when a Participant has already committed to license Essential Claims to Implementers (see Section IV.A). Unlike an "exclusion," where the Participant must affirmatively communicate that it is "opting out" of the disclosure requirement, no communication is generally required for an "exemption." The following is an example of an exemption:

> *The SDO's disclosure obligation as to a particular Essential Claim under Sections III.A.1 and III.A.2 is satisfied if the Patent Holder has made a Licensing Commitment consistent with the SDO's Licensing Commitment requirements for Essential Claims covering the Draft Standard.*

However, since there are other important terms of a patent license in addition to royalties, some SDOs do not permit disclosure exemptions even where the patent holder has committed to license Essential Claims on a RAND basis. SDOs that are primarily concerned with avoiding royalty-bearing licenses may prefer to offer an exemption to encourage Patent Holders to agree to license Essential Claims on a RANDz basis.

The rationale for the exemption discussed in this Section is analogous to the language regarding "blanket disclosures" discussed in Section III.C.3 above. In that case, an otherwise noncompliant Patent Disclosure is excused if the Participant has made the required Licensing Commitment, whereas in this case the obligation to make a Patent Disclosure is excused if the Participant has made such a Licensing Commitment.

3. *Exceptions ("Negative Disclosure")*

Some SDOs do not have a disclosure requirement but do impose a Licensing Commitment. If a Participant is unwilling to license certain Essential Claims consistent with the SDO's Licensing Commitment, then the SDO may permit the Participant to disclose such Essential Claims and thereby avoid any Licensing Commitment with respect to such Essential Claims, as reflected in the language below. Not all SDOs are willing to allow Participants to avoid their Licensing Commitments in this way.

> *Within the period for review of a Draft Standard [1], each Participant shall submit to the SDO a Patent Disclosure covering all Essential Claims Controlled by the Participant for which it will not make licenses available on terms consistent with this Policy. Such Participant shall not be required to grant licenses under such disclosed Essential Claims.*

Note that there is generally a fixed period in which a Participant must disclose a Patent likely to have Essential Claims that the Patent Holder is unwilling to license consistent with the SDO's Licensing Commitment requirement. The period is generally triggered by an event relating to the final approval or ratification of a Draft Standard.

Some may feel that the ability to opt out of an otherwise mandatory Licensing Commitment in this manner lessens the value of the Licensing Commitment. Other Participants view this feature as desirable (for example, to protect against situations in which a Standard exceeds the breadth anticipated by the Participant and encroaches on Claims that are core to the Participant's business, or where another Participant makes a Contribution for the sole purpose of gaining licenses under the Participant's Essential Claims).

Some SDOs, however, may only want to be informed of Claims that are likely to create patent blocking issues for Implementers of its Standards. These SDOs may view the potential for patent-blocking problems to be relatively unlikely when all Participants are willing to license Essential Claims consistent with the SDO's Licensing Commitment requirements. Exceptions allow these SDOs to focus disclosures on only those limited patents identified by Patent Holders unwilling to license consistent with the SDO's Licensing Commitment requirements.

Further, exceptions are also often accompanied by a requirement to disclose with more specificity the relationship between particular Claims in the identified patent and particular portions of the Draft Standard.

E. DURATION OF PATENT DISCLOSURE OBLIGATION

SDO Participants may generally withdraw from the SDO and/or particular Working Groups at any time. A Participant's disclosure obligation should continue during the entire period of its Participation in the SDO, as reflected in the language below:

A Participant's disclosure obligations under Section III.A shall terminate:

[upon its withdrawal from the SDO]

and/or

[with respect to Essential Claims relating to a particular Standard, upon its withdrawal from the relevant WG].

As reflected in the first clause above, a Participant's disclosure obligations terminate upon its withdrawal from the SDO. In the second clause above, a Participant's disclosure obligations with respect to a particular Standard terminate upon its withdrawal from the relevant Working Group.

The SDO may wish to address the possibility of a prospective Participant transferring patents containing Essential Claims in anticipation of joining the SDO (see Section III.A.1). While an SDO might be concerned about a Participant withdrawing and then filing patent applications to cover aspects of a Standard initiated during its period of Participation, imposing a duty to disclose after withdrawal from the SDO is generally viewed as unnecessarily burdensome on Patent Holders. This concern is often addressed in the Licensing Commitment (see Section IV.E.1.a), which may require a withdrawing Participant to continue to offer licenses with respect to Essential Claims covering Standards developed during its period of Participation in the SDO.

F. POTENTIAL CONSEQUENCES OF NON-COMPLIANCE WITH DISCLOSURE OBLIGATIONS

In the event that the Patent Holder pursues claims of patent infringement against an alleged infringer (i.e., an Implementer), the Patent Holder may find itself in a position where it must respond to the following allegations raised by the alleged infringer: (i) the SDO's IPR Policy requires disclosure of Essential Claims owned or controlled by the SDO's Participants, and (ii) the Patent Holder, as a Participant in the SDO, did not disclose its Essential Claims and therefore failed to comply with its disclosure obligations under the SDO's IPR Policy. Such allegations may suggest to a court that the Patent Holder improperly sought to exploit its patents. If the alleged infringer's defense is successful, the court may determine that the Essential Claims are unenforceable against the alleged infringer and any products compliant with the Standard at issue.

The U.S. Court of Appeals for the Federal Circuit has addressed this issue in at least three decisions over the past 15 years.

- ***Qualcomm Inc. v. Broadcom Corp.*, 548 F.3d 1004 (Fed. Cir. 2008)**. This case involved the IPR Policy of the Joint Video Team (JVT) SDO. In reviewing the IPR Policy, the court found that it provided "no express requirement to disclose patents unless a member submits a technical proposal" but nonetheless found that the informal expectations and norms of the SDO required members to make disclosures "on a best effort basis" and encouraged such disclosures "as soon as possible." As for the scope of disclosure, the IPR Policy required disclosure of patents that "reasonably might be necessary" to practice the Standard at issue (H.264). The court found that the Patent Holder (Qualcomm) had not disclosed two of its patents that "reasonably might be necessary" to practice the H.264 standard and, as a result, held that the two undisclosed patents could not be enforced against any H.264-compliant products.
- ***Hynix Semiconductor Inc. v. Rambus Inc.*, 645 F.3d 1336 (Fed. Cir. 2011)**. *Hynix* involved the same Joint Electron Devices Engineering Council (JEDEC) IPR

Policy at issue in *Rambus, Inc. v. Infineon Tech. AG*, 318 F.3d 1081 (Fed. Cir. 2003), which is discussed briefly in the Preface of this book. The court explained that the JEDEC IPR Policy required JEDEC Participants to disclose pending applications and issued patents "with claims that a competitor or other JEDEC member reasonably would construe to cover the standardized technology." In contrast to *Qualcomm*, the court found that the Patent Holder (Rambus) had not breached the disclosure obligation because Rambus's patent claims that were pending while it participated in JEDEC "were not reasonably necessary to practice the standards." It is worth noting that the court reached this conclusion even though Rambus had prosecuted patent claims after withdrawing from JEDEC that were found to be reasonably necessary to practice the standards at issue.

- ***Core Wireless Licensing S.A.R.L. v. Apple, Inc.*, 899 F.3d 1356 (Fed. Cir. 2018)**. At issue in *Core Wireless* was whether the prior owner of the patent-in-suit (Nokia) had breached the disclosure obligations contained in the ETSI's IPR Policy. The IPR Policy required that each ETSI member "shall use its reasonable endeavours to timely inform ETSI of essential IPRs it becomes aware of" and further provided that any member submitting a technical proposal "shall, on a bona fide basis, draw the attention of ETSI to any of that member's IPR which might be essential if that proposal is adopted." The court found that Nokia breached its disclosure obligation because it did not disclose its standards-essential patent until five years after adoption of GPRS, the ETSI Standard at issue. And on remand, the district court held that the patent-in-suit could not be enforced against products practicing the GPRS standard because Nokia (and its successor in interest to the patent-in-suit, Core Wireless) had

> obtained an "unfair competitive advantage" (e.g., through "extract[ing] licenses from industry participants") and "inequitably benefit[ed]" from its untimely disclosure.

In sum, Patent Holders should exercise diligence in ensuring that they comply with the disclosure obligations under an SDO's IPR Policy. They may otherwise face difficulty when attempting to enforce Essential Claims against alleged infringers (implementers) after adoption of the Standard, as well as liability under antitrust, contract, and other laws.

SECTION IV

Licensing Commitments and Licensing Statements

As defined in Section I, a Licensing Commitment is an obligation arising under an SDO policy requiring a Participant to grant licenses under its Essential Claims. A Licensing Commitment is not itself a license grant. It is merely an obligation to grant a license on terms such as RAND or RANDz.

In contrast, a Licensing Statement is a writing containing an affirmative statement in which a Participant makes a Licensing Commitment or otherwise discloses the general nature of the terms on which it would be willing to grant licenses under its Essential Claims. However, some SDOs impose Licensing Commitments without requiring any particular Licensing Statement (for example, the Licensing Commitment may be embodied in the SDO's organizational documents, bylaws, Participation Agreement, or the like). Again, a Licensing Statement generally does not constitute the grant of a license, but generally states the nature of the terms (e.g., RAND or RANDz) on which the Participant commits to grant licenses.

A. LICENSING COMMITMENTS

It is important for Participants to understand their Licensing Commitments so that they do not commit to grant more license rights than they intend or become involved with standards development activities that may require them to grant licenses that they did not contemplate. Patent Holders must weigh the potential benefit of fully exercising patent rights against the benefit of promoting the standard, the industry, and their own business prospects. It is equally important for Implementers to understand the range of license terms and conditions they can generally expect Participating Patent Holders to offer. Implementers generally do not want to invest in the development and deployment of standards-based products if they believe that they will not be offered acceptable patent licenses. The SDO, in creating its Policy, must find a satisfactory balance between the interests of the Patent Holders that participate in and contribute to the Standard, and the interests of the Implementers, whose adoption of the standard is vital for the standard's success.

In practice, not all Patent Holders may require Implementers to obtain a license under their Essential Claims, even if permitted to do so under the Policy and even if they have submitted Licensing Statements to the SDO.[1]

1. *How a Licensing Commitment Arises*

A Participant's Licensing Commitment may arise in various ways. As discussed in detail below, a Participant may be required to undertake a Licensing Commitment when it joins an SDO or a Working Group of an SDO, when it submits a Contribution, or when it submits a Licensing Statement. Some SDOs do

---

1 Some refer to these nonenforcing patent holders as "sleeping dogs". *See*, e.g., Jorge L. Contreras, *Fixing FRAND: A Pseudo-Pool Approach to Standards-Based Patent Licensing*, 79 ANTITRUST L.J. 47, 62 (2013).

not impose any obligation on Participants to make any Licensing Statement or to undertake any Licensing Commitment, although most do impose some form of Licensing Commitment.

As noted above, a Licensing Commitment is not an actual license and generally does not include all the terms that the Patent Holder may include in the licenses it offers to prospective licensees. The Licensing Commitment may, however, prescribe the general nature of some of the terms and/or prohibit other terms. The terms and conditions not expressly covered by the Licensing Commitment are typically negotiated on a bilateral basis between Patent Holders and Implementers,[2] subject to any overarching requirements in the Licensing Commitment that the resulting license be "reasonable" and "nondiscriminatory."

Some SDOs also require different Licensing Commitments depending on a Participant's level of participation or authority within the SDO. For example, Participants who are part of the SDO's "promoter group," "steering committee" or "architecture board" may be required to grant licenses on RANDz terms, whereas more general Participants may be permitted to grant RAND licenses.

The Licensing Commitment is often stated as an absolute (i.e., that the Participant must grant the required licenses). However, it is reasonable to require that such licenses be granted only upon a request by a potential licensee and upon the conclusion

---

2 While negotiations are often bilateral, proposals have been made regarding the possibility of joint or collective negotiation of RAND licensing terms, particularly royalty rates. *See* Jorge L. Contreras, *Aggregated Royalties for Top-Down FRAND Determinations: Revisiting 'Joint Negotiation,'* 62 Antitrust Bull. 690–709 (2017). In a 2007 FTC/DOJ Report, *Antitrust Enforcement and IP Rights: Promoting Innovation and Competition*, the agencies observed that "joint negotiation of licensing terms by standard-setting organization participants before the standard is set can be procompetitive." Such negotiations are unlikely to constitute a per se antitrust violation. The agencies will usually apply a rule of reason analysis when evaluating these joint activities.

of bilateral negotiations. It would be unreasonable for a Participant to be required to seek out its own licensees in this context, or to extend offers before being requested to do so.

2. *Covenant versus License*

Note that, in some instances, a Participant may be permitted to elect to structure these grants of rights as covenants (similar to that described in Section IV.C.3 below) rather than licenses. Some commentators maintain, however, that a Participant offering a covenant should also offer a license as an alternative to permit bilateral negotiation. In any case, any such covenant must still meet all of the requirements of the SDO's Licensing Commitment.

3. *Open-Source Software Considerations*

A company joining an SDO should consider how the SDO's patent policy will affect its business model. For example, the open-source software development model has emerged in various standards-setting environments. If a client plans to implement a standard with open-source software, counsel should consider the interplay between the open-source license commitment the client may have and the SDO commitment it may have. Today there are many open-source implementations of RAND-based standards, although the authors are not aware of the circumstances under which these implementations are being practiced. The leading open-source development organization, the Open Source Initiative (OSI), has noted that all approved open-source licenses must include patent rights on a royalty-free basis without the need for individual licensing negotiations.[3]

Similarly, if the SDO wants to attract software developers including open-source developers, it may consider the interplay between the SDO's commitments, the rights of Patent Holders,

---

[3] https://opensource.org/node/906.

open-source license commitments, and the incentives to innovate within the scope of the standardization activity. Distributors of all products, including those involving open-source software, must also understand that permitted license limitations may affect their ability to distribute products as they might otherwise prefer to do. In addition, the SDO should seek to balance the interests of Implementers (who may rely on differing business models) and the rights of Patent Holders (who may also rely on different business models) in developing its IPR Policy in order to attract a balance of stakeholder interests.

4. *Basic Terms of the Licensing Commitment*

In some SDOs, the Licensing Commitment is as simple as a commitment to grant licenses on RAND or RANDz terms and conditions. Other SDOs require or permit the Licensing Commitment to contain some or all of the terms described below, and many SDOs expressly permit the inclusion of such terms as part of their RAND Licensing Commitment.

As shown in the sample clause below, the Licensing Commitment can specify: (a) which Essential Claims must be licensed, (b) the monetary terms of that license, (c) the scope of the required license grant, and (d) to whom such licenses must be granted.

> *Participant shall, [upon request], [grant/offer] to any [Implementer/Participant] a nonexclusive, [worldwide], nontransferable/nonassignable [perpetual/____-year] [irrevocable] right and license, [without the right to sublicense (except as part of the transfer of [unmodified] products that conform with the Standard)],*
>
> *for [one of the following three options for essential claims]*
>
> *all Essential Claims Controlled by the Participant [or its Affiliates] and described in the accompanying Patent Disclosure [Option 1] OR*

all Essential Claims Controlled by the Participant [or its Affiliates] [covering any element of the Draft/Final Standard] [Option 2] OR

all Essential Claims Controlled by the Participant [or its Affiliates] that cover such Participant's Contributions [if those Contributions are subsequently incorporated into a Final Standard] [Option 3]

under [one of the following two monetary consideration options]

RAND terms and conditions OR RANDz terms and conditions.

To make [have made], use, sell [have sold or distribute], offer to sell [market/promote], [rent/lease, and import [and otherwise dispose of] products that implement [Mandatory Portions of] the relevant Standard [for the purpose of complying with the Standard] or [to the extent that the product complies with the Standard].

a. Which Essential Claims Must Be Licensed?

Option 1: Limited to Essential Claims in the Patent Disclosure. Option 1 is used when a Licensing Statement accompanies a specific Patent Disclosure. It is generally limited to the Essential Claims set forth in the Patent Disclosure. Without more, this Option does not obligate the Patent Holder to license any Essential Claims that it may Control but that it has not disclosed. If the SDO wishes to impose a Licensing Commitment that would encompass as many of the Patent Holder's Essential Claims as possible, it must therefore have a Patent Disclosure requirement that encompasses these Essential Claims (but see discussion in Section III.D relating to disclosure obligations that may be overly broad).

Option 2: Any Claims That Are Likely to Be Essential to the Developed Standards. Option 2 requires that a license be granted under any Essential Claims that the Participant Controls, irrespective of whether the Participant is aware of the Essential Claims and irrespective of whether or not any of the Essential Claims have been disclosed. This requirement could cause problems if one Participant intentionally inserts a technical proposal into a Draft Standard knowing that it is covered by a different Participant's Essential Claims simply to obtain a license to that Participant's patents.[4] This issue may be assuaged by providing each Participant with adequate time to review the Draft Standard and to "opt out" of its Essential Claims (if this option is permitted—see Section III.D) or by prohibiting Participants from knowingly submitting Contributions that are covered by Essential Claims of others, without identifying those Essential Claims.

Option 3: Essential Claims Covering Its Own Contributions. Option 3 covers a Participant's commitment regarding any Essential Claims it Controls that cover its own Contributions, whether or not the Participant is aware of the Essential Claims and whether or not those Essential Claims have been disclosed. In general, a Participant may be more willing to make a RAND Licensing Commitment under Option 3 early in the standards-development process. Some SDOs treat Licensing Commitments for Essential Claims covering a Participant's own Contributions differently than Essential Claims covering other technology included in a Standard. The rationale is that a Participant has control over the technology that it chooses to propose for inclusion in a standard but does not have control over the intellectual property that other Participants may Contribute.

4 This practice has been referred to as "guerilla standardization." *See* Josh Lerner & Jean Tirole, *Standard-Essential Patents*, 123 J. Political Econ. 547, 566–67 (2015).

For example, a Participant may be required to license its Essential Claims under RAND terms, unless its Essential Claims cover a Contribution submitted by that Participant, in which case the Participant is required to license those Essential Claims on a RANDz basis. Other permutations are possible where, for example, a Participant has no Licensing Commitment unless it makes a Contribution, in which case the Participant's Essential Claims covering its Contribution are required to be licensed on a RAND or a RANDz basis.

If a Participant's Contribution(s) are not included in the Final Standard, the justification for licensing Essential Claims covering them is eliminated (and one could argue that such Claims are no longer Essential Claims). See Option 2 above.

b. Which Standards Documents Should Be Covered?

Because implementation of a Standard usually occurs after the Standard is finalized, it may be appropriate to limit the Licensing Commitment to Final Standards. However, if implementations of Draft Standards will be possible and desired by the SDO, or if substantial work within the SDO will proceed based on a Draft Standard, then it may be appropriate for the SDO to require that Licensing Commitments extend to Draft Standards. However, this may discourage participation in the SDO if it is perceived that Licensing Commitments will be required and effectuated before the scope of expected licenses is finalized.

Before extending the Licensing Commitments to cover Draft Standards, the SDO should consider the risk of "forking" or "splintering" the Standard. That is, the SDO should consider how licensing unapproved standards embodied in or derived from Draft Standards may lead away from and hinder the success of the Final Standard. It may be appropriate to provide an experimentation, but not a production, license for Draft Standards. This will allow Implementers to develop and test the early versions of the Standard but not to commercialize them.

c. Control over Essential Claims

Licensing Commitments should generally only cover Claims "Controlled" by the Participant or its Affiliates, because it might be difficult or impractical for the Participant to commit to license Claims that it or an Affiliate did not Control. However, an SDO may wish to address instances relating to Essential Claims Controlled by companies that are owned by several Participants jointly (but in which no one Participant has a majority ownership position) (See Section III.A.1, Disclosure of Claims Controlled by Participant.) In such a case, these minority owners may not have sufficient legal right to cause such a jointly owned entity to make the desired Licensing Commitment.

If an SDO is concerned about the possibility that Essential Claims may reside in such entities, it may wish to consider imposing strong disclosure obligations relative to third-party Essential Claims (since such minority-owned entities would be classified as third parties for purposes of this Policy). If such Claims are disclosed, then Participants may ascertain whether licenses are available. However, minority owners may have insufficiently detailed knowledge of the jointly owned entity's patent portfolio to trigger an obligation to disclose. See Section III.A.3.

d. To Whom Must Licenses Be Granted?

Members-Only or All Implementers. SDOs must decide who will benefit from the Participants' Licensing Commitments—other Participants, or all Implementers. Many SDOs seek to benefit all Implementers of a Standard. This approach is viewed by many as fostering widespread adoption of a Standard. Some SDOs, however, limit Licensing Commitments to other Participants, and Implementers who are not Participants cannot rely on such Licensing Commitments. Such limitations may be imposed because Participants may fear granting licenses to non-Participants that have no Licensing Commitments of their own. These restrictions may also encourage membership in the SDO by attracting Participants who seek licenses under the relevant Essential Claims. This limitation is seen more in SIGs than in "traditional" SDOs.

This being said, if the Policy permits the Patent Holder to include a reciprocity provision in its license (see Section IV.A.2 below), the Patent Holder can obtain a reciprocal license (i.e., limited to Essential Patents) from any non-Participant the Patent Holder chooses to license. Consequently, Patent Holders would have an incentive to license both Participants and non-Participants even if the Policy imposes a Licensing Commitment only with respect to Participants. However, absent such a Licensing Commitment, non-Participants are not guaranteed that the Patent Holder will offer any license at all.

If it is anticipated that a Standard may be submitted to another SDO that does not have this limitation, the SDO, in the Policy, may wish to consider extending the benefit of licenses to all Implementers. Another possibility would be to add a provision that would convert the Licensing Commitment to cover all Implementers in the event that the Standard is contributed to such other SDO.

Level Discrimination. When a Licensing Commitment requires, expressly or implicitly, a Patent Holder to grant licenses to all Implementers of a Standard, must the Patent Holder actually grant such licenses, or is it sufficient to grant licenses only to licensees at a particular level in the supply chain (e.g., end product manufacturers) and then to refrain from suing others who might infringe the Essential Claims? This practice is known as "level discrimination" and is popular among certain Patent Holders because it facilitates seeking a royalty to the producer of the highest-value product (e.g., a smartphone manufacturer versus a chip manufacturer), thereby increasing the amount of revenue that might be targeted for licensing from a particular standardized product. While early Licensing Commitments clearly required Patent Holders to grant licenses to "all applicants," some later SDOs have been less specific about this requirement, leading commentators to question whether level discrimination is restricted under licensing or the "nondiscrimination" prong of the RAND commitment.[5] While the meaning of the Licensing Commitment of SDO policies that are not specific has been a matter for litigation, SDOs that wish to more clearly define the universe of Implementers to which Patent Holders are obligated to grant licenses can do so, and some SDOs have in fact done so.[6]

e. Monetary Consideration

This clause specifies the nature of the financial terms that a Patent Holder must offer to Implementers. In some SDOs, this is the only requirement contained in the Licensing Commitment, and is thus very important.

All licenses granted under RAND and RANDz terms must be "reasonable and nondiscriminatory." The choice between RAND and RANDz determines whether monetary compensation may be required under licenses that are granted. Some SDOs allow Patent Holders to select whether they are willing to undertake a RAND commitment, a RANDz commitment, or no commitment at all.

---

5 *See*, e.g., Jorge L. Contreras & Anne Layne-Farrar, *Non-Discrimination and FRAND Commitments*, *in* Cambridge Handbook of Technical Standardization Law: Competition, Antitrust, and Patents 186, 200-02 (2017), Jorge L. Contreras, *Sometimes FRAND Does Mean License-to-All*, Intell. Asset Mgt. (2020), https://papers.ssrn.com/sol3/papers.cfm?abstract_id=3889813.

6 *See*, e.g., IEEE Policy, *supra* note 11, Sec. 6.2, providing that a patent holder will "make available a license for Essential Patent Claims to an unrestricted number of Applicants on a worldwide basis" where "Applicant" means "any prospective licensee for Essential Patent Claims."

Policy Factors Regarding RAND versus RANDz. Patent Holders often desire to retain flexibility to charge reasonable royalties or fees when they license Essential Claims. Patent Holders, in some circumstances, place primary importance on their ability to use their patents defensively—to enable access to patents controlled by others—and their defensive positions may be enhanced by their right to charge royalties. For other Patent Holders, generating revenue from their patent portfolios is an important part of their business model. These Patent Holders may not Participate or make important Contributions to an SDO if they do not retain the right to license their Essential Claims for reasonable royalties or fees.

In some situations, however, SDOs and Implementers believe that royalty-bearing patent licenses will unduly delay or impede the adoption of the standard. Patent Holders that Participate and Contribute to the development of a standard are frequently Implementers as well. Those Patent Holders sometimes favor a RANDz policy if they believe that the possibility of royalty-bearing licenses will impede either their own ability to implement or use the Standard or the adoption of the Standard by others (which may be as important to their business interests as patent licensing). Where the possible imposition of royalties is likely to affect adoption negatively, SDOs sometimes opt for a policy with RANDz Licensing Commitments.

Recognizing that the specific facts surrounding the development of each Standard may affect whether a Participant desires to make a RAND or a RANDz Licensing Commitment, some SDOs may adopt a flexible approach. Such SDOs may permit Patent Holders either to select from a menu of Licensing Commitment options or select a different option on a Working Group-by-Working Group basis. These flexible approaches are described in more detail below in connection with the acceptance of a Licensing Commitment in Section IV.C.

The Meaning of RAND. Most SDOs do not specify the level of royalties or other monetary compensation that meets the definition of "reasonable" for any given standard or technology. Not surprisingly, this situation has led to disputes in which parties disagree whether the amount demanded by a Patent Holder, or which an Implementer is willing to pay, are, in fact, reasonable. Ultimately, a neutral third party—a court or an arbitrator—may need to resolve the question of whether a license has been offered on RAND terms.[7]

Some SDOs, in an effort to offer greater clarity regarding suitable methods for calculating RAND royalties that comply with their policies, have included more robust discussions of RAND in their policies. For example, the IEEE Standards Association (IEEE-SA) offers the following guidance:

> *"Reasonable Rate" shall mean appropriate compensation to the patent holder for the practice of an Essential Patent Claim excluding the value, if any, resulting from the inclusion of that Essential Patent Claim's technology in the IEEE Standard. In addition, determination of such Reasonable Rates should include, but need not be limited to, the consideration of:*
>
> - *The value that the functionality of the claimed invention or inventive feature within the Essential Patent Claim contributes to the value of the relevant functionality of the smallest saleable Compliant Implementation that practices the Essential Patent Claim.*

---

7 *See*, e.g., Microsoft Corp. v. Motorola, Inc., 2013 WL 2111217 (W.D. Wash. Apr. 25, 2013), aff'd, 795 F.3d 1024 (9th Cir. 2015) (court adjudication of a FRAND royalty for Motorola's H.264 and 802.11 SEP portfolios); Realtek Semiconductor, Corp. v. LSI Corp., 2014 WL 2738216 (N.D. Cal. June 16, 2014) (jury determination for FRAND rate for LSI's 802.11 SEPs).

- *The value that the Essential Patent Claim contributes to the smallest saleable Compliant Implementation that practices that claim, in light of the value contributed by all Essential Patent Claims for the same IEEE Standard practiced in that Compliant Implementation.*
- *Existing licenses covering use of the Essential Patent Claim, where such licenses were not obtained under the explicit or implicit threat of a Prohibitive Order, and where the circumstances and resulting licenses are otherwise sufficiently comparable to the circumstances of the contemplated license.*[8]

RAND and Royalty Stacking. When a large number of Essential Claims cover the same Standard, Implementers may be faced with seeking licenses from multiple Patent Holders. In such cases, even though individual royalty rates may separately appear to comply with an SDO's RAND Licensing Commitment when compared to historical bilateral license rates, the aggregate of these individual royalties may, in the aggregate, become burdensome and exceed the value of the standard. This problem has been referred to as "royalty stacking."[9] In such cases, approaches such as patent pools have been considered, though it is unclear whether pools ultimately help or exacerbate royalty stacking in practice. Counsel must carefully assess the various risks and benefits of such approaches, a discussion of which is beyond the scope of this Guide.

f. Scope of License

Geographic Scope. Licensing Commitments often require the license to be "worldwide." However, "worldwide" does not

---

8 *See* IEEE Policy, *supra* note 11, Sec. 6.2.

9 *See*, e.g., Microsoft Corp. v. Motorola, Inc, 795 F.3d 1024, 1031 (9th Cir. 2015), Ericsson v. D-Link, 773 F.3d 1201, 1209 (Fed. Cir. 2014).

necessarily mean that all worldwide rights are licensed under a single license or to each prospective licensee. Implementers may not want licenses to make, use, sell, etc., the standardized technology throughout the world and may seek licenses for only those regions where the Implementer anticipates practicing the Essential Claims. Patent Holders may also want to offer customized terms for practicing Essential Claims in different regions. This type of strategy, however, may raise questions about reasonableness and nondiscrimination if manufacturers in one jurisdiction are subject to substantially different terms from those in another.[10]

Some SDOs may use the terminology "throughout the world" or "in any country" in the same context.

Rights Granted. The U.S. Patent Act, U.S.C. Title 35, grants five exclusionary rights to the owners of patents, namely, the rights to make, use, sell, offer to sell, and import. Unless otherwise stated, Licensing Commitments would generally require that each of the five statutory rights be included in each license granted. But conceivably Licensing Commitments could specify that not all five rights must be granted in a single license, such that a Patent Holder might offer different licenses covering more specifically enumerated rights.

Some SDO policies incorporate rights in addition to those specifically enumerated under the Patent Act. For example, it is not unusual to include express "have made" rights in Licensing Commitments. In certain industries, such as the semiconductor industry, it is reasonably common for semiconductor enterprises to contract with third-party manufacturers known as

[10] At least one U.S. district court has held that RAND license terms must apply to all similarly-situated licensees worldwide, other than entities that focus exclusively on a local market. TCL v. Ericsson, 2017 WL 6611635, at *31-32 (N.D. Cal. Dec. 21, 2017), vacated on other grounds by 943 F.3d 1360 (Fed. Cir. 2019).

foundries to produce components or products. Express "have made" rights enable a licensee to use a foundry to develop the standardized components or products on behalf of the licensee. Because this right extends benefits to a third party, it is not unusual for the "have made" right to be carefully delimited.

- The Licensing Commitment in some cases assures licensees that they will have the rights to use third-party distributors that are not separately licensed by the Patent Holder. Such Licensing Commitments include either "have sold" or "distribution" rights. In the case of software-related standards these terms can be confusing because third-party distributors would generally need the rights to "make" copies of the software and the Licensing Commitment usually does not make it clear that the right to distribute includes a limited right to make copies for the specific licensee's end users. Some of these concerns are handled by including a limited sublicense in the Licensing Commitment as discussed below in Section IV.A.1.k.
- Licensing Commitments also occasionally include a right "to market" or the right "to promote." It is not clear how these terms differ from the right to "offer to sell" and probably should be avoided.
- Sometimes Licensing Commitments include the rights to "rent" or "lease." In the United States these rights are not explicitly described in the Patent Act, and are more typically related to copyrighted works (see U.S. Copyright Act Sec. 106(3)). However, such SDOs should be clear about the meaning of such terms, particularly when they may be applied to patents and patent claims.
- Licensing Commitments may also attempt to clarify that any license offered by the Patent Holder must permit the licensee to dispose of any Implementation that is

subject to the license. Such a statement may be intended to express a broad permission to commercially exploit a patented article. However, it is not always clear what is intended by the term "dispose of," and for that reason an SDO should include this right in its Licensing Commitment only after careful consideration and preferably with additional clarification of the intent.

Scope of Use/Implementations Covered. This clause describes the implementations that are covered by the license grant. Because Essential Claims may cover only Mandatory Portions of a Standard (including, possibly, Mandatory Portions within the Optional Portions), it is reasonable to limit the Licensing Commitment to Mandatory Portions. A requirement to license Essential Claims under this Policy should be limited to a license required for conformance with the Standard, and should not cover product features not required by the Standard.

Some SDOs address a similar issue by defining a "Compliant" or "Licensed" Product as one that functions, in relevant part, according to the Standard, and accordingly, the scope of the license is limited to Implementations only as incorporated into such Compliant or Licensed Products. Some SDOs also expressly provide that Licensing Commitments must apply to partial implementations of a Standard. One reason this is expressly included is to more clearly allow Implementers to create a component that may be added to others to create a full implementation. SDOs that wish to require full compliance with the Standard in all instances should clearly state this in their policies.

g. Nonexclusivity

Perhaps the most common term included in a Licensing Commitment is nonexclusivity. The licenses offered by the Patent Holder must be nonexclusive to enable broad implementation of the Standard.

h. Nontransferability

Some Licensing Commitments may permit a Patent Holder to offer licenses that are nontransferable or nonassignable. There may be a number of terms in the license that the Patent Holder believes are material to the license agreement with a specific licensee and therefore the Patent Holder does not want the license to be assigned or transferred without its knowledge and consent. Some licenses that are not transferable or assignable do include limited provisions permitting a licensee to transfer or assign its license upon notice to the Patent Holder and with its prior consent.

i. Duration

In a perpetual license, the license of each Essential Claim extends for the life of the applicable patent, unless there is some limiting condition expressed. Implementers often desire a perpetual license because they may not want to invest in a standardized technology believing that the license terms are acceptable, only to find out after the license terminates that the new terms offered by the Patent Holder are not acceptable to the licensee. At that point the Implementer may feel committed to the standardized technology and the Patent Holder's leverage in future licensing negotiations may be increased unduly. Patent Holders may, however, prefer to retain the flexibility to offer licenses on different terms and conditions as the market for a standardized technology matures, to the extent doing so is compatible with the Patent Holder's obligation to offer licenses on nondiscriminatory terms. To do so, license durations of five, seven, or ten years are common. SDOs need to balance the interests of all stakeholders when deciding whether the license granted pursuant to a Participant's Licensing Commitment must be perpetual.

If a license is not perpetual, the term must either be specified by the SDO as part of its Licensing Commitment, or may be unspecified and thus left to bilateral negotiations between the Patent Holder and licensee. Note, however, that if duration is left to the parties, the Patent Holder may not discriminate among licensees in terms of different license durations. Additionally, the Patent Holder cannot collect royalties on patents after their expiration.[11]

j. Irrevocability

Patent licenses offered in connection with a Participant's Licensing Commitment may include termination clauses (including defensive termination or suspension as discussed below). One exception is a license containing an irrevocability clause. Implementers may desire irrevocable licenses under Essential Claims to ensure the greatest certainty regarding their ability to continue to develop products that conform to a given Standard.

Some Policies include Licensing Commitments that require licenses to be irrevocable, but also state that the license may be subject to other terms such as reciprocity and defensive suspension. It is unclear whether, under such Policies, the Licensing Commitment would obligate the Patent Holder to offer a license that did not allow the Patent Holder to terminate the license if the licensee (a) materially breached its obligations, or (b) brought a lawsuit against the Patent Holder involving Essential Claims covered by the defensive termination provision of the license agreement. Any Licensing Commitment that requires the license to be irrevocable should specify whether there are any exceptions under which the license may be terminated. If such exceptions are not specified, then the license may not be terminable, even upon a breach.

It is important to note that an irrevocable license is different from an irrevocable Licensing Commitment (see Section IV.C.5.a).

---

11 Kimble v. Marvel Entertainment, 576 U.S. 446, 465 (2015).

k. No Sublicensing

Most Licensing Commitments expressly permit the Patent Holder to prohibit sublicensing. This means that a licensee does not have the right to sublicense to others the rights it has received. Other parties desiring a patent license must seek a license directly from the Patent Holder. Patent Holders typically wish to negotiate each license so that it can be tailored to address the specific situation with each licensee. However, some Patent Holders are willing to provide to licensees sufficient rights to distribute their own products through their normal distribution channels to the licensee's intended end users without having all of the distributors and end users requiring their own individual patent licenses. For this reason, some Licensing Commitments make it clear that the license will not be sublicensable except as part of a transfer of a product that conforms to the Standard.

As mentioned above, a license conveying the right to "distribute" can be confusing because it is not a statutory patent right, though it is a statutory right under the U.S. Copyright Act (see Section 106). Some have interpreted the right to "distribute" under a patent license to permit a licensee to sublicense its rights so as to allow its distributors to distribute the licensee's products to end users and to permit end users to use such products. SDOs should ensure that their Licensing Commitments are clear with respect to any sublicensing rights that a Patent Holder may or must grant in its licenses and should not presume that a Licensing Commitment that includes the rights to "distribute" but is otherwise nonsublicensable will be understood in the same way by all Participants and Implementers.

In some cases, the SDO may wish to require that sublicensing of Essential Claims be permitted only if the associated products are unmodified by downstream distributors/users. This measure is sometimes viewed as a means of preventing the licensee from acting as a "foundry" or "cleansing" agent for third-party products that would not otherwise be licensed.

5. *Reciprocity*

A reciprocity provision in an SDO policy permits a Patent Holder to condition its license of Essential Claims on the licensee's granting some form of license back to the Patent Holder and/or to others to the licensee's own Essential Claims.[12] Such "reciprocity" provisions are often included in licenses granted under RAND and RANDz terms. However, if an SDO wishes to avoid any ambiguity regarding the "reasonableness" of reciprocity terms when used by Patent Holders, the Policy should either expressly permit or prohibit such terms. The following language addresses two potential reciprocity requirements in a Licensing Commitment:

> ***Bilateral Reciprocity****. A license granted under this Policy may require that the licensee grant a reciprocal license to the licensor under any Essential Claims Controlled by such licensee. OR*
>
> ***Unilateral Reciprocity****. A license granted under this Policy may require that the licensee grant a reciprocal license to all other Implementers that so request under any Essential Claims Controlled by such licensee[provided that the Implementer agrees to reciprocity with the licensee [and other Implementers]] [and that all such Implementers shall be deemed to be third-party beneficiaries of this grant].*

a. Bilateral Reciprocity

In many cases, a Patent Holder may offer a RAND or RANDz license conditioned on the licensee agreeing to grant a

---

12 Reciprocity is similar, but not identical, to a grantback clause, under which a licensor requires a licensee to grant it a license to any improvements made by the licensee to the licensed technology. See U.S. Dept. Justice and Fed. Trade Comm'n, Antitrust Guidelines for the Licensing of Intellectual Property, Sec. 5.6 (2017).

corresponding RAND or RANDz license to the Patent Holder under its own Essential Claims. Reciprocal licenses can take many forms. They may require the licensee to grant a license to the Patent Holder covering Essential Claims relating to the same standard, Essential Claims covering a broader group of standards, patents not essential to a Standard, or the licensee's entire patent portfolio. Likewise, the licensee may or may not receive "credit" for its reciprocal license (thus reducing its payments to the Patent Holder). And the Patent Holder may or may not have the right to sublicense the rights granted to it by the licensee. Some variants of these reciprocity requirements may be found to be anticompetitive, and some Patent Holders have been found liable for imposing excessive reciprocal licensing requirements in their licenses.[13]

SDOs that permit reciprocity should recognize the possibility that one Patent Holder could potentially convert the SDO's RAND policy into a RANDz policy (that is, by requiring that licensees grant it reciprocal licenses on a RANDz basis). For example, the ITU-T has permitted a Patent Holder making a RANDz commitment to condition it on bilateral reciprocity on a RANDz basis, but if a reciprocating licensee wants to make its Essential Claims available on a RAND basis, then the original Patent Holder can change its commitment for that specific licensee to a RAND one.

b. Universal Reciprocity

Some SDOs seek to promote the adoption of their Standards by permitting Patent Holders to condition their patent licenses on the licensee granting a reciprocal license of its Essential Claims

[13] For example, in 2015 China's National Development and Reform Commission ("NDRC") found that Qualcomm violated China's Anti-Monopoly Law by, among other things, requiring licensees to grant Qualcomm royalty-free licenses of their non-essential patents covering wireless telecommunications technologies.

not only to the Patent Holder, but to all other Implementers that may request a license. In effect, such a clause requires all licensed Implementers to license all other existing and prospective Implementers on a reciprocal basis. Such "universal" reciprocity provisions avoid the perceived unfairness of a licensee granting rights to a third party who might assert Essential Patents against the Patent Holder.

6. *Defensive Suspension*

A defensive suspension clause permits a licensor to suspend (or terminate) a license if the licensee asserts a claim of some kind against the licensor. The following language authorizes a Patent Holder to include a definitive suspension clause in a license granted under the SDO's patent policy:

> *It is acknowledged that references in this Policy to a license agreement containing RAND or RANDz terms may include a license agreement with [reasonable] "defensive suspension" provisions.*
>
> *"Defensive Suspension" means that the license granted by the Participant, and any commitment to license by the Participant with respect to the Participant's Essential Claims, [is automatically suspended/may be suspended at the Participant's option] if the licensee [first] [initiates/threatens] or participates in a legal action [for patent infringement] against [Participant/any Implementer][on account of its compliant implementation of the Standard/any SDO Standard] [under the licensee's Essential Claims].*

Definitive Suspension Generally. Unlike reciprocity, in which a licensee may not acquire a license at all unless the licensee agrees to offer a reciprocal license, a licensee can acquire and benefit from a license with a defensive suspension provision so long as the licensee does not take certain actions against the licensor (or, in some cases, other Implementers). Consequently, from a contractual perspective, reciprocity is often considered a condition precedent whereas defensive suspension is often considered a condition subsequent—the difference potentially reflecting damages that may be accrued by the licensor based on the commencement of the infringing activity. Another difference between reciprocity and defensive suspension is that reciprocity in most cases requires that the licensee be willing to grant a license under its Essential Claims for implementations of the same Standard on a reciprocal basis, whereas defensive suspension may be triggered by various acts of the licensee that may or may not be limited to Essential Claims and may or may not be based on alleged infringements in an implementation of the same Standard.

Some SDO policies expressly state that a defensive suspension provision is permissible as a RAND term. Other policies are silent as to whether defensive suspension is permitted. A reasonable defensive suspension clause, limited to Essential Claims, generally has been viewed as a permissible RAND term, though this assumption has not been validated through litigation.

Automatic or Discretionary Suspension. Some SDO policies specify whether, upon the occurrence of a defensive suspension trigger, the license will be suspended automatically or at the discretion of the licensor. If the license is suspended automatically, the licensee becomes an infringer as soon as it triggers the suspension. If on the other hand, the licensor has discretion to suspend the license upon the occurrence of such an act, then the licensee may not become an infringer until and unless the licensor notifies the licensee that the license has been suspended.

Triggering Defensive Suspension. The acts that can trigger the suspension of a license generally involve the licensee initiating a legal action against the licensor or threatening to bring such an action. Depending on the terms of the defensive suspension clause, the legal actions may be based on any type of legal claim or may be limited to situations where the licensee initiates a patent infringement lawsuit against the licensor. Some may view suspension of a RAND license based on any claim whatsoever as being overreaching, and therefore limit the situations in which the licensor may suspend a RAND patent license to situations involving the assertion of patents. Some include further limitations, discussed below, allowing suspension only when the alleged infringing activity relates to Essential Claims and/or the same or related Standards.

As mentioned above, defensive suspension may be triggered by the initiation of a lawsuit or by simply threatening to bring one. It may be difficult to assess what constitutes a "threat" sufficient to trigger the defensive suspension provision. For this reason, some SDOs prefer to require that a lawsuit actually be filed before the defensive suspension can be triggered. Patent Holders may prefer to be able to suspend the license as soon as a licensee threatens to bring a lawsuit as a way to possibly avoid litigation over the potential dispute. In contrast, a licensee may want more clarity over the actions it might take that could result in loss of its patent license to practice the Standard. To avoid showing preferences to licensees or licensors, some SDOs do not specify whether the lawsuit need only be threatened or actually filed and instead leave such details to the individual negotiations among licensees and licensors.

Some SDO policies may provide that the target of the licensee's claims must be the licensor (and may include the licensor's Affiliates) while others may permit terms that broadly cover any Implementer. An SDO permits a defensive suspension provision to be invoked when the licensee takes action against any

Implementer for essentially the same reasons an SDO selects universal reciprocity to encourage acceptable licensing terms among all Implementers of the Standard, not only those that Participate in its development.

Some variations on the scope and triggers for defensive suspension may raise antitrust concerns or questions as to the reasonableness of such provisions under RAND requirements. For example, competition authorities in the United States and Europe have expressed concerns when SEP Holders have attempted to condition the license of Essential Patents to an agreement by the licensee not to assert nonessential patents against the SEP Holder.[14]

Although a defensive suspension provision does not require a licensee affirmatively to grant an express or implied patent license, it can be tantamount to such a requirement, since it effectively prohibits the licensee from asserting its own patents against the licensor.

In an effort to limit the breadth of acts that trigger the suspension of a license, some SDOs limit suspension to claims that a compliant portion of an Implementation of the Standard infringes a patent of the licensee. The licensor would only be able to suspend its patent license if the licensee sues the licensor for infringement on account of the licensor's compliant portion of an Implementation of the same Standard. In other words, the licensor would be unable to suspend the license if the allegedly infringing product were something other than a compliant portion of an Implementation of the Standard, even if the assertion were based on Essential Claims. One benefit of such a provision is that it encourages licensors and licensees to enter into portfolio licenses that cover each other's commercial Implementations, thereby avoiding future conflicts between the

---

[14] *See*, e.g., In the Matter of Motorola Mobility LLC and Google Inc., File No. 121 0120, Docket No. C-4410 (July 23, 2013).

two parties. The drawback of such an approach is that some Patent Holders may be discouraged from participating in the standards development if they cannot retain broad defensive rights with respect to their Essential Claims. However, counsel representing Patent Holders seeking to include broad defensive rights in the licensing of Essential Claims should carefully consider the reasonableness and potential anticompetitive effects of such broad provisions.

Some SDOs develop multiple Standards. Such SDOs may specify that a license may be suspended with respect to a licensee that sues the licensor for infringement based on the licensor's compliant implementation of any of the SDO's Standards, not only the Standard that is the subject of the license (see, e.g., the World Wide Web Consortium patent policy). As mentioned earlier, if obtaining a license is critical to a Licensee's commercial interests, then a defensive suspension provision may be tantamount to a requirement for a reciprocal license. Thus, SDOs that choose to permit suspension of licenses when a licensee sues a licensor for infringement based on the licensor's Implementation of a different Standard than the one to which the license pertained is in effect trying to encourage all implementers of all of the SDO's standards to offer acceptable licenses to all other Implementers. Some Patent Holders may be more likely to participate when policies permit them to retain broad defensive rights, whereas prospective Implementers may be discouraged from adopting a standard if they risk losing licenses to Essential Claims for enforcing a patent with respect to a different standard.

The primary purpose of a defensive suspension provision is to permit the licensor to use its patents defensively in a suit in which the licensor is being accused of infringement. However, some policies are not clear whether such defensive use stems from a licensee initiating a lawsuit against the licensor or whether it might also cover situations in which the licensee has counterclaimed for infringement in a suit first brought by the licensor. For example, a Participant may enter into a RAND license with an Implementer granting the Implementer a license under the Participant's Essential Claims to implement the SDO's Standard. The Participant sues the Implementer for patent infringement on account of a product that does not implement the Standard. The Implementer counterclaims alleging that the Participant is infringing the Implementer's patents. Some SDOs do not view a counterclaim as an offensive tactic justifying the suspension of the Participant's RAND license. These SDOs might clarify in their patent policies that defensive suspension is permissible if the license is suspended only in situations where the licensee initiated the original or first lawsuit. SDOs may likewise clarify whether a counterclaim raised by a licensee in a lawsuit first brought by the Participant/licensor justifies the suspension of a RAND license.

Some defensive suspension policies limit the suspension of a license to those situations in which the licensee sues the licensor only under its Essential Claims with regard to an implementation of the same Standard. Such limited defensive suspension policies have the same effect as reciprocity policies, except that the lawsuit by the licensee becomes a condition subsequent whereas the agreement to reciprocally license Essential Claims is a condition precedent. While this distinction may have some bearing on the damages to which the licensor may be entitled based on when the infringement commenced, the scope of patent rights involved are the same as those covered by a reciprocal license. In some cases, such limited defensive suspension provisions are permitted in lieu of reciprocity so that a licensee is not required to give a reciprocal license to its Essential Claims at the outset, but if the licensee later chooses to sue the licensor under its Essential Claims for infringement based on the licensor's implementation of the Standard, the licensor may suspend its license.

B. OBLIGATION STRUCTURE OF THE LICENSING COMMITMENT

Licensing Commitments, as discussed above, may arise in several ways and may become effective at different points in the standardization process. The SDO Participation Agreement, Bylaws, or operating procedures typically set forth the point at which a Licensing Commitment applies or must be made and when the Licensing Commitment becomes effective. SDOs may employ different combinations of events triggering the acceptance of various Licensing Commitments as well as different combinations of events that render the Licensing Commitment effective.

1. *Events Triggering the Imposition of a Licensing Commitment*

The following language addresses the range of potential events that trigger the imposition of a licensing commitment:

> ***Upon Joining the SDO****. The Licensing Commitment described in [Section IV.A.1] above shall become effective upon a Participant's membership in the SDO.*
>
> ***Upon Joining a Working Group.*** *The Licensing Commitment described in [Section IV.A.1] above shall become effective upon a Participant's joining a specified Working Group.*
>
> ***Upon Submission of a Contribution****. The Licensing Commitment described in [Section IV.A.1] above shall apply with respect to each Contribution made by a Participant.*
>
> ***Upon Submission of a Licensing Statement*** *Each Licensing Statement submitted by a Participant shall describe the Participant's Licensing Commitment [, which shall comply with the requirements of [Section IV.A.1] above].*

Upon Joining the SDO. Some membership-based SDOs provide that Licensing Commitments are made as a condition of membership in the SDO. A Participant must agree to the Licensing Commitment, either by signing a Participation Agreement or by implication as a condition to its Participation in the activities of the SDO.

Upon Joining a Working Group. Not all SDOs require Participants to undertake any Licensing Commitments as a condition of membership in the SDO. However, some of these SDOs do require members that wish to Participate in the SDO's standards development activities to undertake a Licensing Commitment for the work coming out of a specific Working Group before they can join that Working Group. These SDOs presume that those joining Working Groups are the most likely to make Contributions covered by their Essential Claims, or are more likely to Control Essential Claims relevant to the work of the Working Group. SDOs that adopt this approach should be careful that they do not permit non-Working Group members to contribute or indirectly influence the work of a Working Group where they have no Licensing Commitment.

Upon Submission of a Contribution. Some SDOs require Participants to agree to a Licensing Commitment for any Contributions they make.

Upon Submission of a Licensing Statement. In SDOs where the Participation Agreement or Bylaws do not impose a Licensing Commitment as a condition of membership or Participation, Participants may be required to make Licensing Commitments by issuing Licensing Statements at certain stages during the standards development process. This requirement may or may not be triggered by a disclosure of the existence of an Essential Claim. The circumstances under which Licensing Statements must be submitted are discussed in Section IV.C below.

2. *Events That Render Licensing Commitments Effective*

Section IV.B.1 above discusses the circumstances giving rise to Licensing Commitments. This Section IV.B.2 describes specific events that make a Licensing Commitment "effective." That is, the point at which a Patent Holder must offer a license to a Participant or prospective Implementer that requests one. A Participant or prospective Implementer may request a license earlier, but the Patent Holder may not be obligated to provide it until a certain event has occurred.

The following language addresses the range of events that may render Licensing Commitments Effective:

> *The Licensing Commitment described in [Section IV.A.1] shall become effective with respect to a particular Standard upon [approval/ publication] of the relevant [Draft/ Final Standard] [but only if the Participant voted in favor of approving such Standard].*

Approval/Publication of the Standard. The SDO should decide when a Standards Document is in a form that is definitive enough to warrant the imposition of a Licensing Commitment. Most SDOs would be reluctant to impose a Licensing Commitment before a Standards Document is sufficiently mature to avoid additional substantive changes that could have a material effect on the patent claims that would be considered Essential Claims with respect to such Standards Document. In most SDOs, the requisite level of stability is deemed to occur upon publication or approval of the Standards Document.

Before making a Licensing Commitment effective upon the approval of Draft Standards, the SDO should consider the risk of "forking" or "splintering" the Standard. That is, the SDO should consider how licensing unapproved standards embodied in or derived from Draft Standards may lead away from and hinder the success of the Final Standard. It may be appropriate to provide an experimentation, but not a production, license for Draft Standards. This would allow Implementers to develop and test the early versions of the Standard but not to commercialize them. Compare Section IV.A.1.h relating to scope of the license for Draft/Final Standards.

Approval before Essential Claims are Covered. Another option is to require the Participant to approve a Standard before its Essential Claims are covered by a Licensing Commitment. However, leaving the determination of whether or not the Licensing Commitment is made to the discretion of the Participant could lead to behavior in which a Participant deliberately refrains from approving a Final Standard in order to avoid making a Licensing Commitment (e.g., if sufficient votes to approve the Standard have already been obtained). Therefore, this formulation is not common.

3. Establishment of Licensing Commitments by Working Groups

SDOs that wish to allow each Working Group to choose its own Licensing Commitment policy may provide their Working Groups with two or more Licensing Commitments to choose from. These SDOs often develop many standards and include Participants from many different industries. As such, they realize that one Licensing Commitment policy may not meet the needs of each of its standards development efforts. However, these SDOs also want to ensure that there are certain acceptable

Licensing Commitments for each of their standards development efforts.

The following language addresses the establishment of Licensing Commitments by Working Groups:

> *At the time a Working Group is chartered, the proposal to form the Working Group must specify the Licensing Commitment that will be applicable to all Participants in the Working Group. [Such Licensing Commitments must include the requirements of [Section IV.A.1].]*
>
> *[A Working Group may not change its Licensing Commitment requirements without closing and submitting a new charter.]*

Range of Licensing Commitments. The Licensing Commitment options that may be implemented by Working Groups may include particular elements discussed in Section IV.A.1 that the SDO deems important to the adoption of its Standards and to its Participants.

Limitations on Changing Licensing Commitment. SDOs that permit Working Groups to choose which policy option they will use regarding Licensing Commitments generally do not want those Licensing Commitments to be changed after the Working Group has commenced its work. Such SDOs often require that the Licensing Commitment be included in the Charter of the Working Group so that anyone who joins or participates in the Working Group is advised of the applicable Licensing Commitment. To ensure that Participants in the Working Group are aware of any change in the applicable Licensing Commitment, SDOs often require the Working Group to re-charter with the policy for the new Licensing Commitment before any changes can go into effect.

4. *Reduction of Licensing Commitment*

In some cases, an SDO may permit Participants to "opt out" of or reduce ("opt down" from) Licensing Commitments with respect to particular Standards or other circumstances. For example, if a Participant Controls Essential Claims that it does not wish to license under the applicable SDO License Commitment, it might be able to exclude those Essential Claims by notifying the SDO by a certain deadline. Sometimes, election of such options has consequences for the Participant's future participation in the SDO.

Some Patent Holders, concerned with committing to license patents without knowing what the final specification is, and before knowing what the implicated patents are (recognizing that piecemeal searching of large portfolios may be burdensome), may seek robust opt-out or opt-down provisions. Often such Patent Holders are concerned that a competitor may contribute the Patent Holder's own technology to the Standard without the Patent Holder's knowledge or consent, which can be particularly of concern if the SDO's Licensing Commitment is based on a RANDz approach. Other parties, concerned with developing and investing in a standards-development effort and then discovering Essential Claims for which there is no Licensing Commitment and for which the Standard may be blocked, may favor no opt-out or opt-out early in the development process or opt-out after successive drafts with respect to only new subject matter in each such draft. Some SDOs do and others do not condition continuing membership in the working group and/or in the SDO on whether a Participant fully commits all of its Essential Claims (e.g., without opt-out or opt-down). Some SDOs apply different opt-out (opt-down) limitations depending on a Participant's level of Participation in the relevant Working Group.

The following language addresses opt-out and opt-down limitations:

> *Within ___ days following [approval/publication] of a [Draft] Standard, a Participant shall have the right to submit to SDO a list of Essential Claims that such Participant elects to exclude from its Licensing Commitments under this Policy. The Participant shall not be obligated to comply with such Licensing Commitment with respect to all Essential Claims so disclosed before the end of such ___-day period.*
>
> *Within ___ days following [approval/publication] of a [Draft] Standard, a Participant shall have the right to submit to the SDO a list of Essential Claims that such Participant elects to license on a [RAND] rather than a [RANDz] basis under its Licensing Commitments under this Policy. The Participant shall be entitled to so reduce such Licensing Commitment with respect to all Essential Claims so disclosed before the end of such ___-day period.*

These provisions enable Patent Holders to deny (reduce) their Licensing Commitment with respect to otherwise Essential Claims. Some SDOs do, and others do not, allow opt-out (opt-down). Those that provide for opt-out (opt-down) typically allow for a time period(s) during which opt-out (opt-down) must be exercised. For example, some SDOs require opt-out (opt-down) within a fixed period after the Final Standard is published, while others adopt a process in which exercise must occur within a specified period after the technology of the Essential Claim is first published in any Standards Document (draft or final) or the Working Group's charter. Opt-out (as described in Section IV.D.4.a above) enables the Patent Holder to choose not to license identified Essential Claims to Implementers. Opting-down from a royalty-free commitment to a reasonable royalty commitment, however, should still enable Implementers to acquire licenses, albeit under less favorable terms.

Some Patent Holders, concerned over any agreement to license Essential Claims without knowing what the Final Standard will be, and before knowing what the implicated patents are (in that piecemeal searching of large portfolios may be burdensome), may seek robust opt-out or opt-down provisions. This may also be the case when, as discussed above, technology covered by the Patent Holder's Essential Claims are contributed by a Participant other than the Patent Holder. Other Participants, concerned with developing and investing in a Standard and then discovering Essential Claims for which there is no Licensing Commitment and under which the Standard may be blocked, may favor no opt-out or opt-out early in the development process, or opt-out after successive drafts with respect only to new subject matter in each such draft.

5. *Effect of Opt-Out and Opt-Down*

Some SDOs do, and others do not, condition continuing membership in the Working Group and/or in the SDO on whether a Participant fully commits all its Essential Claims (e.g., without opt-out or opt-down). Some SDOs apply different opt-out (opt-down) limitations depending on a Participant's level of Participation in the Working Group.

The following language addresses the range of effects of opt-out and opt-down reductions:

> ***No Effect****. A Participant who "opts out" of its Licensing Commitments in accordance with the provisions of Section*

IV.B.4 above may continue to participate in the SDO and its Working Groups without penalty.

Loss of Benefit of Licensing Commitments. *No Participant shall be required to grant any license to any Participant who has elected to "opt out" of its Licensing Commitments under Section IV.B.4 above [with respect to the Standard as to which such Participant has opted out].*

Removal from SDO Activities. *If requested by [the SDO/ any other Participant in the WG], a Participant who "opts out" of its Licensing Commitments under Section IV.B.4 above shall cease its Participation in [the SDO/ all Working Groups engaged in work on Standards Documents implicated by such opt-out].*

C. LICENSING STATEMENTS

Some SDOs do not impose uniform Licensing Commitments on Participants, as described in Section IV.A above, but instead require Participants to state their intentions with respect to licensing of particular Essential Claims in a written (and binding) Licensing Statement. Licensing Statements may be required to have varying levels of detail, as discussed below. In addition, some SDOs may require that Licensing Statements disclose or characterize certain minimum licensing terms, and thus embody Licensing Commitments. Other SDOs, however, impose no particular Licensing Commitment and allow Participants to choose any form of licensing, or to decline to license at all, so long as this intention is clearly expressed in a Licensing Statement. In such cases, it is understood that the SDO may attempt to remove or work around patented technologies as to which adequate RAND or RANDz licensing commitments have not been made.

1. *Elements and Types of Licensing Statements*

The following clauses addresses the range of potential Licensing Statements:

> ***Licensing Commitment.*** *Each Licensing Statement shall set forth the Participant's Licensing Commitment with respect to the Essential Claims subject to the Licensing Statement.*
> ***Essential Claims When Accompanying a Patent Disclosure.*** *If a Licensing Statement accompanies a Patent Disclosure, the Licensing Statement shall relate to the Essential Claims disclosed in such Patent Disclosure.*
> ***No Licensing Commitment.*** *A Participant may state in its Licensing Statement that it is not willing to license any, or certain, of its Essential Claims, or that it is not currently prepared to make any commitment with respect to licenses of such Essential Claims.*
> ***Nonassertion Covenant.*** *[A Participant may elect to make a written, [unconditional] commitment not to assert any Claims described in its Licensing Statement against any Implementer of the relevant Standard. Such statement shall be treated as a Licensing Commitment under this Policy as long as it otherwise complies with the requirements of any Licensing Commitment imposed on the Participant.]*

Licensing Commitment. The terms of the Licensing Commitment disclosed in the Licensing Statement should be consistent with the SDO's Policy and may correspond with some or all of the terms described in Section IV.A.1 above. In many SDOs, a simple statement agreeing to license on RAND or RANDz terms suffices to satisfy the Licensing Commitment.

Essential Claims When Accompanying a Patent Disclosure. This Clause is used when a Licensing Statement accompanies a specific Patent Disclosure. It is generally limited to the Essential

Claims identified in the Patent Disclosure. A Licensing Statement accompanying a Patent Disclosure is usually requested or required only where the Patent Holder is not already obligated through the Participation Agreement, Bylaws, or other operating document to undertake a particular Licensing Commitment.

No Licensing Commitment. Some SDOs allow Participants to avoid or delay making a commitment regarding their licensing intentions (i.e., a statement that the Participant does not intend to grant licenses under the relevant Essential Claims). If this approach is allowed, then the Participant makes no Licensing Commitment in its Licensing Statement.

Nonassertion Covenant. A few SDOs expressly recognize that a non-assertion covenant made by a Participant may satisfy the SDO's Licensing Commitment requirements. Unlike licenses that are granted pursuant to Licensing Commitments, however, such nonassertion covenants are often evidenced as public statements published by the Participant, either on its website, on an SDO licensing page, or elsewhere. As such, such covenants are typically not signed by the parties or negotiated on a bilateral basis (though technically there is nothing to prevent parties from negotiating nonassertion covenants in the same manner as they would negotiate license agreements, or from posting generally applicable license terms on their websites or elsewhere). Like license agreements, nonassertion covenants must include any specific terms required by the SDO and, if required by the SDO, must be made on RAND, RANDz, or other required terms. Thus, such a covenant may be recognized by an SDO as an alternative way of satisfying a Licensing Commitment. Most such covenants contain terms and conditions, such as those described in Section IV.A.1. Just as with licenses, whether any such covenant satisfies a RAND or RANDz requirement is a case-by-case determination.

2. *Timing of Licensing Statements*

The following language addresses the potential timing of Licensing Statements:

I. **An Initial Licensing Statement Must Be Made When a Participant Joins the SDO. Upon joining SDO or the relevant Working Group, each Participant shall submit to the SDO a Licensing Statement in the form required by this Policy.**

II. **Licensing Statements [Must/May Be Made] When a Corresponding Patent Disclosure Is Made. Each Patent Disclosure submitted by a Patent Holder [shall/may] include a Licensing Statement that covers the Claims disclosed in such Patent Disclosure.**

III. **Licensing Statements Must Be Made When a Draft Standard Reaches a Particular Stage of Advancement. Each Patent Holder [that has [materially/ actively] Participated in the development of a Standards Document] must make a Licensing Statement no later than [____days before the Standards Document becomes a Draft Standard/Final Standard.]**

IV. **Licensing Statements Must Be Made When Requested by the SDO.**

   A. ***Call at the Request of a Participant.*** Any Participant that believes in good faith that another Participant(s) Controls an [Essential Claim] covering any [Mandatory Portion/portion] of a Standards Document may request in writing that the SDO seek to obtain a Licensing Statement from such Participant(s). The requesting

Participant must state the specific item that it believes may be covered by the Claim.

B. ***Issuance of Licensing Call Following Request.*** Promptly following receipt of such a request, the SDO shall request in writing that each Participant that is the subject of such a request confirm or deny that it Controls the alleged Essential Claims and, if so, that it submit a Licensing Statement with respect thereto. [The SDO shall not disclose the identity of the Participant who initiated the request under this paragraph].

C. ***Responsibility to Respond.*** All Participants to which a Licensing Call is directed [shall] [are encouraged to] respond in writing as requested no later than [x] days following the SDO's delivery of the Licensing Call.

D. ***Licensing Statements Are Optional.*** Patent Holders are encouraged to disclose to the SDO whether they are willing to license their Essential Claims that may cover one or more aspects of a Standard under the Licensing Commitment parameters (e.g., RAND, RANDz) permitted under the SDO's policy [if any].

[The SDO shall issue a Licensing Call to the Participants in the relevant Working Group no later than ____ days before such Licensing Statement is due.]

1. *An Initial Licensing Statement Must Be Made When a Participant Joins the SDO.* Some membership-based SDOs provide that Essential Claims must be licensed as a condition of membership. In some SDOs, these requirements may differ depending on whether or not a Participant is a member of the relevant Working Group.

These requirements may be contained in the Participation Agreement, Bylaws, Operating Procedures or similar documents.

2. *Licensing Statements [Must/May Be Made] When a Corresponding Patent Disclosure Is Made.* SDOs may require that a Licensing Statement accompany any Patent Disclosure. This requirement gives other Participants and Implementers notice of the Patent Holder's Licensing Commitment and possibly a description of the terms that will (or may) be applicable to the disclosed Essential Claims if a Standard Document becomes a Draft Standard or Final Standard. However, it is not always the case that Licensing Statements must accompany Patent Disclosures, and in some cases the SDO may simply wish to give Participants information about potentially relevant Essential Claims, but not to require Patent Holders to make a Licensing Commitment at that time.

   Use of the term "may" instead of "shall" makes this an optional statement, which may be preferred by some SDOs. (See discussion above regarding "Licensing Statement.")

3. *Licensing Statements Must Be Made When a Draft Standard Reaches a Particular Stage of Advancement.* In some cases, Participants may be required to make Licensing Statements at certain stages before a Standards Document becomes a Final Standard, even if they are not concurrently required to make a Patent Disclosure (that is, a Licensing Commitment may be required even if the Participant is not aware of Claims that are likely to be Essential Claims with respect to the Standard in question).

   If the language "Participated in the development of a Standards Document" is used, the SDO must decide whether there should be any threshold on the Patent Holder's involvement in the development of the Standards

Document before it is required to submit a Licensing Statement. Without any modifier, it is possible that any involvement, however slight (even passive observation), will give rise to this obligation.

A requirement of "active" participation requires some affirmative level of contribution to the development effort beyond passive observation. A requirement of "material" participation requires a still greater level of contribution but may be the subject of some dispute. While the term "material" is frequently used in legal documentation, there are not well-understood conventions for its interpretation, and some level of ambiguity is inherent in the term's use. In many cases, an SDO will deem a Participant who joins a Working Group to be an active participant in that Working Group.

A number of SDOs, instead of using terms such as "material" or "active," define specifically the activities giving rise to this obligation. See definition of "Participation."

In order to be most useful, Licensing Statements should be made, to the greatest extent possible, within a reasonable period of time before approval of the relevant Draft Standard or Final Standard, so that the members of the relevant approval body have time to consider its implications (such as an unwillingness to license). If an SDO has multiple levels of "Final Standard," then the appropriate stage at which this Licensing Statement should be submitted may vary.

4. *Licensing Statements Must Be Made When Requested by the SDO.* In some cases, an SDO may request that one or several Participants submit a Licensing Statement.
    a. *Call at the Request of a Participant.* An SDO may issue a Licensing Call upon the request of a particular Participant who believes in good faith that another

Participant holds Essential Claims that have not been disclosed.

b. *Issuance of Licensing Call Following Request.* While this obligation may provide greater security and comfort to Participants making such requests, the SDO should be cognizant of the legal implications of assuming such obligations and the potential liability to the SDO arising from a failure to comply with such obligations. Conversely, an SDO that does not commit to maintain the confidentiality of the identity of such Participants may discourage Participants from coming forward with such information to avoid becoming subject to an infringement suit by the Patent Holder.

c. *Responsibility to Respond.* Many SDOs do not make these types of formal requests. If a Patent Disclosure is made and no Licensing Statement is received by the SDO, then, depending on a consensus of the SDO Participants, the Standards Document may still be approved as a Final Standard, or the standards activity might be stopped or modified. SDOs that proceed to publish a standard where no Licensing Statement is submitted under these circumstances typically include a disclaimer in the Final Standard regarding the Patent Disclosure and the lack of Licensing Statement.

d. *Licensing Statements Are Optional.* Some SDOs may not wish to require their Participants to submit Licensing Statements. These SDOs may, however, make requests from time to time of their memberships at different levels of activity during standards development. Even in these cases, it may be a good practice to state that such disclosures are "encouraged," even if not required. Even if there is a requirement to disclose patents, an SDO that does not require any Licensing Commitment or Licensing Statement is assuming certain risks. First, Participants may Control Essential Claims of which the Participants are not aware and the SDO may promulgate the Standard incorporating the covered technology. And second, in any event, with no Licensing Commitment, the Participant may choose not to license or to license at unreasonable rates. However, it also can be burdensome to encourage or require Licensing Statements when the Patent Holder is not aware that it holds one or more Essential Claims. Patent Holders may be concerned that other companies will then seek to include technology covered by its Essential Claims in the Standard in order to gain access to it.

3. *Format of Licensing Statements*

The following language addresses options for whether Licensing Statements are required or optional:

Option 1: The SDO Requires Use of a Specified Disclosure Form. *All Licensing Statements must be made using the Licensing Statement Form that can be found at [www.sdo.org/licensingstatements]. Each section of the Licensing Statement Form that is applicable must be completed in order for the Licensing Statement to be accepted by the SDO. The SDO reserves the right to change the format and/or content of the Licensing Statement Form at any time by posting a revised Licensing Statement Form at the Web address listed above. All Licensing Statements made [more than 30 days after the posting of a revised Licensing Statement Form/with respect to any Standards development project commenced after the posting of such* *revised Licensing Statement Form] must use such revised Licensing Statement Form in order to be accepted.*

Option 2: The SDO Makes Available a Specified Licensing Statement Form but Does Not Require Its Use*. Licensing Statements must be in writing and submitted to the [address] set forth in Section [___] of this Policy and must include all information required by this Policy, but may otherwise be made in the manner selected by the Participant. If they so desire, Participants may, but are not required to, submit Licensing Statements using the Licensing Statement Form that can be found at [www.sdo.org/licensingstatements]. Use of this Form is optional, and neither its use nor nonuse will benefit or prejudice any Participant.*

Option 3: The SDO Has No Specified Licensing Statement Form*. Licensing Statements may be made in the manner selected by the Participant; however, all Licensing Statements must be clear and must include all information required by [Section IV.C.2/this Policy].*

Option 1: The SDO Requires Use of a Specified Disclosure Form. Some SDOs, such as those handling numerous Licensing Statements or those that conduct a review and approval of each Licensing Statement, may wish to require that Licensing Statements be made using a uniform Licensing Statement Form. Such a form makes it easier for the SDO to compare Licensing Statements or to publish them in an automatic manner.

If a Licensing Statement Form is required, the SDO should make it readily available, such as posting it on a website or including it in the Policy. Since a web posting is relatively easy to update, this approach is recommended over inclusion in the Policy, which may require more procedural steps to revise. The preparation of a mandatory form (or the revision of such a form) should have appropriate legal review to ensure that it is consistent with the applicable provisions of this Policy.

The SDO may find it necessary to update its Licensing Statement Form from time to time. If the form is revised by the SDO, the SDO should provide sufficient notice of the revision to the Participants and make the revised Licensing Statement Form available to the Participants. However, so as not to disrupt Licensing Statements that were in preparation at the time of the revision, it is recommended that a reasonable "Grace Period" be allowed between the posting of the revised Licensing Statement Form and the requirement that the revised Licensing Statement Form be used for all Licensing Statements. Following the expiration of this Grace Period, the SDO should no longer accept Disclosures made on outdated Licensing Statement Forms and should notify the submitter of the rejection of the form (see Section VI.B.1).

It is recommended that the SDO clearly provide the version number or the revision date on all Licensing Statement Forms so that both the Participants and the SDO can easily distinguish which form is in effect.

The preparation of a mandatory form (or the revision of such a form) should have appropriate legal review to ensure that it is consistent with the applicable provisions of this Policy. Appendix A sets forth some drafting considerations for Licensing Statement Forms.

If the Licensing Statement Form is changing because of a material change in the Policy, the SDO may not want the new Policy to apply to current Standards projects (regardless of when they will be completed) because it might be perceived to change the rules midstream and possibly impact different Patent Holders differently. Thus, if the SDO changes its Policy materially and a new Licensing Statement Form is adopted, some SDOs require only that the new Licensing Statement Form begin to be used with respect to new projects.

Option 2: The SDO Makes Available a Specified Licensing Statement Form but Does Not Require Its Use. The SDO may wish to allow Participants to make Licensing Statements in whatever reasonable manner they desire, subject to their compliance with the other submission requirements (such as the proper submission address and the details required in any submission). This freedom is often desired by large Participating Organizations that belong to numerous standards organizations, and that wish to make Licensing Statements in an in-house format.

Even if Participants are given the flexibility to make Licensing Statements in the manner in which they choose, the SDO may find it useful to make a "sample" or "template" Licensing Statement Form available. Such a Form can provide a useful starting point for Licensing Statements and may help to ensure that Participants structure their individual Licensing Statements in a way that presents all of the information required by the Policy. However, if the Licensing Statement Form is not *required,* then the SDO should not penalize Participants who fail to use it, provided that their customized Licensing Statements supply all required information.

Option 3: The SDO Has No Specified Licensing Statement Form. The SDO may wish to allow Participants to make Licensing Statements in whatever reasonable manner they desire, subject to their compliance with the other submission requirements (such as the proper submission address and the details required in any submission).

This freedom is often desired by large Participating Organizations that belong to numerous standards organizations, and that wish to make Licensing Statements in an in-house-format.

4. Content and Specificity of Licensing Statements

It is important that each Licensing Statement include all information that the SDO deems to be relevant to an effective assessment of the Essential Claims covered by such Licensing Statement. Licensing Statements generally disclose the Patent Holder's commitment with regard to (i) the Standard or portion of a Standard to which the Licensing Statement applies, (ii) whether it will license its Essential Claims, and (iii) the terms and conditions under which such licenses will be granted (e.g., RAND or RANDz). While different SDOs may include more or fewer terms than those outlined above, many SDOs seek a limited obligation in the Licensing Statement and leave the parties to negotiate other terms later. The following policy language addresses the content and specificity of a Licensing Statement:

Each Licensing Statement shall contain the following information:

Name of Submitter: *The name of the Participant and, if an individual, his or her Sponsor, as well as the name and contact information for one or more knowledgeable individuals at such Sponsor (name, e-mail address, and telephone number).*

I. *Patent Details*: The patent/serial number [and issuance/filing date] of each patent or [published] patent application that contains Essential Claims being disclosed [and, if such patent contains both Essential Claims and other Claims, the number of each Essential Claim].

II. *Standard Details*: The specific Standards Document covered by each Essential Claim covered by the Licensing Statement. [If a Standard

has multiple independent portions, some of which are not covered by the disclosed Claim, then the specific subsection of the Standard that is covered by the disclosed Essential Claim shall also be listed.]

III. ***Licensing Terms.***

[Option 1—Menu of Options] Which of the following Licensing Commitments the Patent Holder elects with respect to the Essential Claims covered by this Licensing Statement:

A. The Patent Holder will grant a RANDz license.
B. The Patent Holder will grant a RAND license.
C. The Patent Holder is unwilling to grant license according to the provisions of either a. or b. above.

[Option 2—Textual Description] Each Licensing Statement shall describe the Patent Holder's Licensing Commitment [on the terms described in Section IV.A.1].

IV. The Licensing Statement [[shall]]/may] also include the following additional information:

______________________________.

1. *Patent Details*: Some SDOs require that the patent numbers accompany each Licensing Statement. This is not required by all SDOs, and the SDOs that do not mandate the disclosure of the patent number typically allow the disclosure of the patent number as optional information on the Licensing Statement. See Commentary in Section III.C.2.
2. *Standard Details.* Just as it is important for Patent Disclosures to map to particular Standards Documents and sections of Standards Documents, some SDOs require that Licensing Statements also map to particular Standards

Documents and sections of Standards Documents. This level of specificity is not always necessary, however, for SDOs that wish to impose broader Licensing Commitments, such as those that cover all of an SDO's standards, or all Standards Documents in which a Patent Holder participated. Broader or blanket Licensing Requirements obviate the need for specific disclosure of Standard details and also avoid situations in which a Patent Holder's intentional or inadvertent failure to update a Licensing Statement to include a new version of a Standard Document results in no Licensing Commitment as to that new version.[15]

3. *Licensing Terms.* Some SDOs that offer a form for Licensing Statements often provide a menu of Licensing Commitment options from which the Patent Holder must select as discussed in Section IV.B.1.d. In most cases the forms that offer such menus of options include an option for RANDz and RAND. Many SDOs that provide menu options in Licensing Statements also permit Patent Holders to indicate their unwillingness to license, in which case the SDO may investigate means of avoiding the relevant Essential Claims.

   Other SDOs allow Patent Holders to describe their individual Licensing Commitments, if any, in whatever manner they choose. Such "free-form" disclosure may be attractive to some Patent Holders because it allows them flexibility and consistency with their own licensing practices. Moreover, it would enable the Patent Holder to use the same internal form document for each SDO in which

---

[15] For example, in Commonwealth Sci. & Indus. Research Organisation (CSIRO) v. Cisco Sys., 809 F.3d 1295 (Fed. Cir. 2015), the patent holder committed to license a key patent covering the WiFi standard on RAND terms. However, its licensing statement only covered the 802.11a version of that standard but did not apply to subsequent versions of the standard such as 802.11g, -n or -ac.

it participates. However, such flexibility can introduce inconsistency regarding the obligations of different Patent Holders within the same SDO and can make it more difficult for Implementers to understand what licenses they are entitled to receive.

4. *Other Information—Royalty Rates.* While the first edition of this Guide was being prepared, a significant debate emerged in the industry regarding the ability of SDOs to require Patent Holders to disclose the maximum royalty rates that they would charge for Essential Claims.[16] One SDO, VITA, did adopt such a requirement and received a favorable business review letter from the U.S. Department of Justice confirming that such a measure could have procompetitive effects.[17] Other SDOs, including IEEE and ETSI, considered such a requirement and opted, instead, to permit, but not require, the disclosure of mandatory royalty rates.[18] While these provisions continue to remain in effect, they are infrequently used.

5. *Who Must Make a Licensing Statement?*

Depending on which clauses the SDO selects for when a Participating Organization must or may make a Licensing Statement regarding Essential Claims, it will also be necessary to select clauses describing who the SDO considers to be an authorized submitter of a Licensing Statement. In addition, if the SDO

---

16 *See* Jorge L. Contreras, ed., *Standards Development Patent Policy Manual*, Appendix A (2007) (discussing the "ex ante" question).

17 U.S. Dept. of Justice, Business Review Letter to VMEbus International Trade Association (VITA) at 3 (Oct. 30, 2006).

18 *See* Jorge L. Contreras, *Technical Standards and Ex Ante Disclosure: Results and Analysis of an Empirical Study*, 53 JURIMETRICS 163, 175–77 (2013).

permits disclosures relating to third-party patents, it should also describe how the SDO will respond.

The following language addresses by whom the Licensing Statement is Made:

1. ***Individual Participants***. *If employed or contracted individuals Participate in the activities of the SDO, they shall be deemed to represent their Sponsors, who [shall be required to make/shall be deemed to have made] the Licensing Statements described above.*
2. ***Requesting Licensing Commitments from Third Parties***. *In the event that a Participant or any other person notifies the SDO that a third party Controls, or may Control, Essential Claims, whether that notification is made in a Patent Disclosure described in Section III.A.3 above or otherwise, then the SDO [may/shall], within ___ days of receipt of such notification, make a written request to such third party for a Licensing Statement covering the relevant Essential Claims. The SDO [may/shall] make available any response received from such third party in accordance with Section IV.D.1 above. Other than making such a request and making any response available in accordance with this Section IV.D.5, the SDO shall have no responsibility to seek a Licensing Commitment from any third party.*

Individual Participants. Most SDOs recognize that Individual Participants in SDO activities may not themselves be authorized to bind their Sponsor organizations. Nevertheless, an SDO may wish to establish that the Sponsor is bound by the Licensing Statements submitted by its Individual Participants. Organizational Participants should thus be careful to institute internal procedures governing the authority of their personnel who attend SDO meetings and submit materials to SDOs, including legal review of documents, such as Licensing Statements, produced and submitted by Individual Participants.

Third Parties. This clause relates to actions that the SDO may take if it receives notification that a third party may hold patents covering the SDO's Standards Documents. Several SDOs, including ETSI and IETF, will respond to such a notification by sending a request for licensing information to the identified third party. Of course, an SDO has no legal authority over nonparticipating third parties and cannot require them to comply with the SDO's licensing or disclosure requirements.[19] Nevertheless, some SDOs may wish to specify what would happen if the SDO does not receive a response to a third-party request within a certain time period. For example, the relevant Working Group may be required to consider the disclosed third-party Claims for a specified period of time to assess whether they will materially affect the viability of the Standard and, if so, to consider whether such Claims may be avoided.

6. *Irrevocability of Licensing Commitments; Withdrawal from SDO*[20]

It generally is understood that the commitments made by Participants in their Licensing Statements are, by their very nature, binding and irrevocable, particularly if others have reasonably

---

[19] The issue of SDO "outsiders," which are not bound by an SDO's licensing commitments, but which may nevertheless hold essential claims, is discussed in Jorge L. Contreras, *When a Stranger Calls: Standards Outsiders and Unencumbered Patents*, 12 J. COMP. L. & ECON. 507 (2016).

[20] Perpetual and/or irrevocable licensing commitments should be distinguished from licensing commitments to grant perpetual and/or irrevocable licenses. See Section IV.A.1 above for a discussion of perpetual and/or irrevocable licenses.

relied on them in ordering their business affairs.[21] However, without specific policy language, some Participants may phrase their Licensing Statements in a tentative manner, stating, for example, that it is merely their "present intention" to grant RAND licenses or that they are "favorably inclined" to do so. With "weasel words" like these, Patent Holders could seek to renege on their commitments to grant licenses on RAND or RANDz terms. What's more, depending on the specificity of Licensing Statements, there is often ambiguity regarding the robustness of a Participant's Licensing Commitment after it withdraws from the SDO. To avoid the ambiguity that could result from these situations, SDOs may wish to include express policy language clarifying the irrevocable nature of the commitments made in Participants' Licensing Statements, and what effect their withdrawal from the SDO will have on such commitments.

The following language offers several options regarding the irrevocability of a Participant's Licensing Commitment:

> ***[Option 1] All Standards Documents.* Licensing Commitments are binding on Participants for the life of the patents in question and encumber the patents containing Essential Claims, regardless of changes in the Participant's participation status or SDO membership with respect to all Standards Documents.**
>
> ***[Option 2] Standards in Which the Participant Participated.* Licensing Commitments shall be irrevocable with respect to all Standards in which the Participant Participated prior to the Participant's withdrawal from the SDO.**
>
> ***[Option 3] Standards Approved prior to Withdrawal.* Licensing Commitments shall**

---

21 *See*, e.g., Contreras, *Market Reliance, supra* note 2 (discussing reliance and promissory estoppel theories in the standards context).

> **be irrevocable with respect to all Standards [published/ approved/approved by the Participant] [within ___ days] before the Participant's withdrawal from the SDO.**
>
> ***[Option 4] Future Standards.* Notwithstanding a Participant's withdrawal from the SDO, such Participant's license grants and Licensing Commitment shall remain in full force and effect:**
>
> i. *for any Essential Claim covering any Contribution made by such withdrawing Participant and incorporated in any Standard (either before or after such withdrawal); and/or*
> ii. *for any Essential Claims covering any Standard approved after such withdrawal, provided that such Essential Claims cover elements of the Standard that are used in a substantially similar manner and to a substantially similar extent with a substantially similar result as such elements were used in a prior Standard for which the withdrawing Participant is obligated to grant licenses un-der such Essential Claims.*

All SDO Standards. Under Option 1, a Participant's Licensing Commitments remain in effect with respect to all Standards Documents produced by the SDO, both before and after a Participant's withdrawal from the SDO. An SDO may wish to clarify that Essential Claims subject to the Licensing Commitment can arise even after a Participant withdraws (e.g., if they are part of a patent family as to which a Licensing Commitment was previously made).

In some cases, SDOs adopting Option 1 may wish to make only certain Licensing Commitments irrevocable. In particular, those SDOs that encourage early disclosure of Essential Claims and an accompanying Licensing Statement that includes a Licensing Commitment may permit such early Licensing Commitments to be altered as the Standard matures. Other SDOs, as discussed in Section IV.B, may delay the effective date of the Licensing Commitment based on the maturity of the Standard being developed.

Standards in Which the Participant Participated. Under Option 2, the Participant's Licensing Commitment is irrevocable with respect to Standards in which the Participant was involved. The level or extent of such involvement is discussed in the definition of "Participate." From the Patent Holder's perspective, this formulation may be desirable because it provides certainty regarding the Standards as to which its post-withdrawal Licensing Commitment will apply.

Standards Approved Prior to Withdrawal. Option 3 is somewhat broader than Option 2, in that the Patent Holder's Licensing Commitment applies to all Standards published or approved prior to the Patent Holder's withdrawal from the SDO, irrespective of its Participation in the specific standards development activity. This formulation provides certainty regarding the Standards as to which the Patent Holder's post-withdrawal Licensing Commitment will apply and does not require Implementers to determine whether or not a particular Holder was involved in a particular standardization activity. However, the SDO should consider the possibility that some Patent Holders could withdraw from the SDO in order to avoid licensing their Essential Claims.

Future Standards. In addition to Options 1–3 above, some SDOs, particularly those that develop multiple standards for multiple technologies, enable the reuse of Contributions made for one standard in other standards, even after a Contributor withdraws from the SDO.[22] Patent Holders, however, may wish to limit the extent of their post-withdrawal obligations and prevent such license obligations from requiring the grant of licenses in contexts that were not originally anticipated.

In some instances, a new or revised Standard may continue to require a feature from a prior version that continues to provide substantially the same function in substantially the same way to achieve a substantially similar result as in the prior version. So that the later version can continue and succeed, a Licensing Commitment with respect to the prior version can be applied to the new version even after the Participant withdraws.[23] If the technology or feature is used in a new way, the Licensing Commitment would not apply. This measure helps to ensure that the new version is no less robust than the prior version with respect to Essential Claims Controlled by a Participant that has withdrawn between two versions of the same Standard and that small, unrelated changes in the standard do not require new Licensing Commitments. However, when a standard does depart from a prior version in a substantial way, the prior commitment may not apply.

D. THE EFFECT OF PATENT TRANSFERS ON LICENSING COMMITMENTS

In the modern technology economy, patents are frequently transferred from one owner to another, through discrete sales of individual patents and portfolios, corporate divestitures and spinoffs, bankruptcy sales, and the like.[24] In this rapidly changing environ-

---

22 Such reuse of contributions is almost always permitted under the copyrights in those contributions, but policies are more varied with respect to patents.

23 Such a clause would have addressed the situation that arose in CSIRO v. Cisco, *supra* note 33.

24 The transfer of standards-essential patents to nonpracticing entities for licensing and enforcement purposes is increasingly common.

ment, it is important to ensure that Licensing Commitments made with respect to Essential Claims remain in place after patents containing those Essential Claims are transferred to new owners, even if those new owners are not Participants in the relevant SDO. Moreover, it is important to ensure that the new owners of such patents are required to comply with such Licensing Commitments, even if they have acquired Essential Claims as part of a much larger acquisition of businesses and technology rights.

There is some indication that, at least in some countries, the new owner of a patent may be liable for a violation of competition law if it does not honor a prior Licensing Commitment made with respect to that patent.[25] However, depending on the country, it is far from clear that the law will automatically apply a prior Licensing Commitment to the new owner of a patent. Thus, SDOs have increasingly sought to ensure that Licensing Commitments "run with the patent" through policy clauses binding on the party originally making the Licensing Commitment.[26] The following policy language seeks to achieve this result:

> *The Participant agrees that any document or other instrument effecting the transfer by the Participant to a*

---

25 *See*, e.g., Negotiated Data Solutions LLC, No. C-4234 at App. D, 2008 WL 4407246 (F.T.C.) (Sept. 23, 2008); Contreras, *Market Reliance*, *supra* note 2, at 499-500 (discussing various instances in which transfers occurred and their effect on underlying Licensing Commitments).

26 *See* Natl. Research Council, Intellectual Property Challenges for Standard-Setting in the Global Economy at 88-93 (Keith Maskus & Stephen A. Merrill eds., 2013) (describing SDO policy approaches to patent transfer), Justus Baron et al., *Making the Rules: The Governance of Standard Development Organizations and their Policies on Intellectual Property Rights*, *in* JRC Science for Policy Report, EUR 29655 at 157 (Nikolaus Thumm ed., 2019) (discussing noncontroversial nature of SDO policy amendments relating to patent transfer). For examples of SDO policies that include such transfer provisions, *see*, e.g., NFC Forum, IPR Policy, Section 3.11 (June 4, 2015), available at https://nfc-forum.org/wp-content/uploads/2013/11/NFC-Forum-IPR-Policy.pdf (last accessed Sept. 14, 2020); ETSI Policy, *supra* note 11, Sec. 6.1bis.

third party of a Patent having Essential Claims, or Control thereof, shall include a provision expressly requiring the transferee to take the patent subject to all Licensing Commitment(s) made by the Participant transferor with respect to such Essential Claims prior to the date of such transfer, and to honor and abide by such Licensing Commitment as though it were the original party making such Licensing Commitment **[1]**, *and to ensure that any further transferee of such patent is subject to the same requirement during the entire term of such patent* **[2]**.

[3] *[The Participant further represents and warrants that it has not and will not transfer or otherwise encumber its patents or patent applications having Essential Claims for the purpose of circumventing the commitment to make disclosures or grant licenses contained in this Policy. Any transfer or grant of exclusive license rights (except for transfers or exclusive license grants pre-dating this Agreement that were not made or granted for the purpose of circumventing obligations hereunder) by a Participant or its Affiliates to a third party of a patent having Essential Claims shall be subject to the terms and conditions of this Agreement, including but not limited to all obligations to grant licenses on RAND/RANDz terms hereunder.]*

1. This clause requires a Participant to ensure that the transferee of any patent subject to a Licensing Commitment takes the patent subject to the commitment and agrees to abide by such commitment. Note that the commitment by the new owner need not be specific to particular Essential Claims—a

blanket acknowledgement and agreement to abide by existing Licensing Commitments may be legally sufficient.[27]

2. This clause ensures that a transferee similarly binds future transferees of the same patent. It is necessary to avoid the elimination of Licensing Commitments through serial transfers.

[27] This concern is particularly acute when Licensing Commitments are undertaken simply by virtue of a company's Participation (rather than Contribution) in a standards activity or by a blanket Licensing Commitment made to an SDO (as opposed to the company's having provided a specific Licensing Statement in connection with a specific, disclosed Essential Claim).

SECTION V

Normative and Informative References

The wide use of references in the development of standards has been described as follows:

> *A specification is rarely developed from scratch: it usually relies on other technologies defined in different specifications. The Working Group has to identify any specifications that define the core technologies of the developed technology.*
>
> *For the Working Group, normative references have an immediate benefit: "Do not reinvent the wheel." Using features already defined in other documents helps to minimize the size of the specification and to avoid ambiguities by rewriting the same concepts.*
>
> *Knowing that a part of a specification is based on another technology is a huge benefit for implementers as it clarifies the implications for conformance. Normative references may help implementers to minimize their work by using conformant libraries already implemented elsewhere.*
>
> *More generally, normative references might help readers understand where the technology is coming from and therefore how to use it in combination with other technologies they may already know.*[1]

[1] W3C Guideline at http://www.w3.org/TR/2005/REC-qaframe-spec-20050817/#reference.

The use of references in Standards Documents, however, can raise a number of issues for SDOs. In particular, SDOs should consider whether patents that cover referenced specifications or other materials (References) should be subject to the SDO's licensing and/or disclosure requirements. What licensing and/or disclosure obligations did those that contributed to the development of the Reference undertake? Will those obligations extend to the Reference if the referencing standard modifies the Reference or includes only portions of it? How should an SDO reference another standard that itself references other standards or specifications? As the practice of building standards on a foundation of References becomes increasingly more prevalent in standards setting, more SDOs are addressing these issues in their Policies.

Additionally, if a reference is informatively referenced some Implementers may not be able to obtain a license at all, even if the Policy seeks to ensure that Licensing Commitments are available for Normative References. When a particular Informative Reference becomes widely adopted by many Implementers it can become a *de facto* requirement of the standard. Patent Holders having Essential Claims that cover such Informative References may permissibly discriminate against certain Implementers, limiting the market opportunities for such Implementers. However, caution should be exercised when deciding whether to identify a referenced document as normative if the technical experts do not believe it really is necessary or it causes the Standard to be overly broad in scope. Moreover, many SDOs expressly exclude Normative References from the scope of their Policy. A concern in excluding technology or other standards that are referenced is that the referencing standard may be unimplementable or impaired without the availability of such necessary resources.

Accordingly, SDOs should consider the intellectual property and other ramifications associated with designating a reference as a Normative Reference or as an Informative Reference.

1. *Claims Expressly Not Covered*

> *Essential Claims shall not include Claims that are infringed by the implementation of technology developed [elsewhere] OR [outside of the Working Group] and merely incorporated by reference in the body of the relevant Standard.*

Some SDO policies make explicit exclusions for Essential Claims that cover References so that such Essential Claims are not subject to the disclosure or licensing obligations of the SDO's policy for the referencing standard.

SDOs opt for exclusions when they choose to defer to the policies in place for the Reference. By doing so the SDO avoids conflicting obligations and/or commitments in connection with the Reference arising from (i) the applicable patent policy for the development of the Reference, and (ii) the patent policy for the development of the referencing standard. The result, nonetheless, can be inconsistent and confusing to Implementers. For example, if the referencing standard is developed under a RANDz policy, Implementers may expect to pay zero royalties, at least for known Essential Claims. However, under the exclusion approach, reasonable royalties may be requested if the References were developed in SDOs with RAND policies. Similarly, Patent Holders subject to the RANDz policy of the referencing standard do not want to be disadvantaged when negotiating with Patent Holders subject to the RAND policy of the referenced standard.

SDOs may also consider whether Licensing Commitments made by Participants for a referencing standard should also apply to Normative References, especially when the referencing standard involves a RANDz Policy. If the SDO developing the referencing standard wants to facilitate implementation on a RANDz basis, extending the Licensing Commitment to

Normative References could be helpful. As discussed above, however, challenges may arise when the policies of the referenced and the referencing Standard are inconsistent, and the authors are unaware of any policy that expressly extends the Licensing Commitment to Essential Claims covering Normative References.

In addition, as suggested above, such a provision can substantially add to the burden on Patent Holders who would have to review (perhaps multiple cascading) referenced standards and make a RANDz Licensing Commitment *vis-à-vis* referenced standards where there may be Patent Holders who are not subject to a similar RANDz Licensing Commitment.

Some SDOs have different policies or Licensing Commitments that apply to different Working Groups. Such SDOs may choose to exclude Claims covering specifications or standards developed by other Working Groups of the SDO when those other documents are merely referenced in standards developed by a different Working Group.

2. *Consistency Required*

> *A reference developed by another SDO may be considered as a Normative Reference only if that SDO's patent policy is consistent with the patent policy applicable to the referencing Standard.*

Some SDOs limit the standards that can be referenced in the SDO's own Standards by requiring that any Normative Reference be developed pursuant to consistent policies, including patent policies. In this way the SDO still avoids conflicts that might arise between various SDO policies. Most of these SDOs, however, do not make it clear whether or not Essential Claims covering a Normative Reference must be disclosed pursuant to the SDO's policy. This lack of clarity can create confusion as to where a potential implementer should look for Patent Disclosures and Licensing Statements, i.e., to the SDO developing the referencing standard or to the SDO or other entity that developed the referenced standard. SDOs that adopt the consistency approach often "qualify" other SDOs after evaluating the consistency between their policies, among other things, and include such SDOs on a publicly available list. References approved by these qualified SDOs may be normatively referenced.[2]

3. *Disclosure Requested*

> *If a Draft Standard contains one or more Normative References to a document published by another SDO engaged in the formulation, development, or publication of standards (whether designated as a standard, specification, recommendation, or otherwise), whether such reference consists of Mandatory, Alternate, or Optional elements then:*
>
> A. *[the referencing SDO] disclaims any duty or obligation to search or investigate the records of any other SDO for IPR or letters of assurance relating to any such Normative Reference; and*
>
> B. *[the referencing SDO's] policy of [encouraging or requiring] disclosure of Essential Claims shall apply; and*
>
> C. *Information as to Essential Claims in the records or publications of the other SDO shall not constitute identification to [the referencing SDO] of a claim of Essential Claims.*

Some SDOs, especially those that obtain Licensing Commitments from Patent Holders in connection with a Patent

---

2 *See* e.g., ITU-T's list of approved SDOs (http://www.itu.int/ITU-T/tsb-director/sdo/qualified.html#Organizations).

Holder's disclosure of Essential Claims, extend their disclosure policies to Essential Claims covering Normative References. In this way, the SDO normatively referencing another SDO's standards can be assured that it will follow the same processes it uses for obtaining Licensing Commitments for Mandatory Portions of its standards. SDOs that require or encourage disclosure with respect to Normative References should disclaim responsibility for ascertaining or identifying Essential Claims disclosed to the other SDO during the development or approval of the referenced standard.

Under these circumstances, a Patent Holder that disclosed its Essential Claims to the SDO that developed the Normative Reference is not relieved of any disclosure obligations it might have to disclose the Essential Claims to the SDO developing the referencing standard and may possibly be required to make a different Licensing Commitment. For those Patent Holders that did not participate in the development of the referenced Standard, this type of policy may prove burdensome (especially if the referenced Standard is large or itself contains Normative References).

SECTION VI

SDO Actions and Responsibilities

The preceding Sections dealt largely with the rights and responsibilities of SDO Participants; this Section VI deals with the duties of the SDO itself. And while some of these duties extend beyond the purview of patents, strictly speaking, they are relevant to implementing an effective SDO patent policy.

A. TREATMENT OF PATENT DISCLOSURES AND LICENSING STATEMENTS

1. *Publication of Patent Disclosures and Licensing Statements*

Option 1: Available to Public

It is acknowledged by all Participants that the SDO [may/will] publish or otherwise make publicly available all Patent Disclosures and Licensing Statements that it receives.

Option 2: Available Only to Participants

It is acknowledged by all Participants that the SDO [may/will] distribute or make available all Patent Disclosures and Licensing Statements to other Participants, but will not otherwise publicly disclose such Patent Disclosures and Licensing Statements.

2. *Retention of Patent Disclosures and Licensing Statements*

The SDO shall make each Patent Disclosure and Licensing Statement applicable to a Standard available in accordance with Section V.A.1 above until the later of the expiration of the Standard and all revisions and derivatives thereof, or the expiration of all Claims contained in such Patent Disclosure.

Where an SDO will make Standards developed under its authority available to the public, that SDO may also elect to make available to the public (e.g., by posting on the SDO website) any Patent Disclosures and Licensing Statements that it receives and accepts (See Section VI.B). This measure helps Participants, Implementers, and users assess the patent landscape.

The SDO shall retain in its [permanent] records a copy of all [Contributions], Patent Disclosures, and Licensing Statements submitted and shall make such records available to Participants upon request (provided that a fee may apply for records retrieval, copying, or similar costs).

Where an SDO elects to make Standards developed under its authority available only to Participants, that SDO will likely also make available only to Participants any Patent Disclosures and Licensing Statements that it receives. Some SDOs may choose an option to do so only upon request. This practice better protects confidential information of Participants that is included in Patent Disclosures and/or Licensing Statements (particularly if patent applications are to be disclosed). This clause may be suitable in cases in which Licensing Commitments are for the benefit of Participants only (see IV.A.1.a above).

[Notwithstanding the foregoing, the SDO shall be free to dispose of any records in accordance with its then-current document retention policy after ____ years from the date of receipt.]

Retaining Contributions, Patent Disclosures, and Licensing Statements for an appropriate time is reasonable practice for an SDO and may help to resolve later disputes among Participants and Implementers.

B. REVIEW OF PATENT DISCLOSURES AND LICENSING STATEMENTS BY THE SDO

1. *Rejection by the SDO*

[With the exception of Blanket Disclosures described in Section III.C.3 above,] any Patent Disclosure that does not contain all information required by [this Policy/ Section III.C.2], and any Licensing Statement that does not contain all information required by [this Policy/ Section IV.C.3 above], shall be rejected by the SDO [with an accompanying explanation]]. **[1]**

[The SDO shall not reject any Patent Disclosure or Licensing Statement due to the inclusion of additional information beyond what is re-quired, provided that such additional information is provided in a manner that does not detract from or obscure the required information.]

1. In order to avoid claims of discriminatory treatment, the SDO should treat noncompliant Patent Disclosures and Licensing Statements consistently. Thus, if noncompliant submissions are to be rejected, then all such noncompliant submissions should be rejected.

Some SDOs whose Licensing Statement Forms provide a list of options from which a Licensing Commitment must be selected explicitly state that the submittal of a Licensing Statement Form without any option selected does not comply with the Policy and will be automatically rejected.

2. *Correction of Clerical Errors*

> *Notwithstanding the provisions of Section VI.B.1 above, the SDO may, in its sole discretion, elect to correct or bring to the attention of the submitter any manifest clerical or typographical errors in any submitted Patent Disclosure or Licensing Statement, rather than reject such Patent Disclosure or Licensing Statement as provided in Section VI.B.1.*

Rejection of a Patent Disclosure or Licensing Statement could be for two reasons: (1) noncompliance with the SDO policy (which includes leaving required fields incomplete), and (2) incorrect data referencing the subject Standard or incorrect data in the contact information.

Rather than reject any Patent Disclosure or Licensing Statement, the SDO may choose to include language in its Policy or operating procedures that permits the staff of the SDO to change certain data contained in fields related to the identification of the corresponding standard or contact information included in the Patent Disclosure or Licensing Statement.

Specifically, in the event of an obvious error such as a misspelling of a word in a document title (e.g., wiring entered as wriing) or a transposition of numbers in the reference document (e.g., 802.11 is entered as 820.11) or a typographical error in the contact information, the staff reserves right to change information for consistency and will notify the submitter of the change. The notification from the SDO to the submitter allows the submitter to accept the proposed correction of the data by the staff, which can expedite the cycle of posting statements and ensures consistency in the posting of data by the SDO.

One consideration in deciding to include such a provision in an SDO policy is to what degree of responsibility staff should be given in ascertaining compliance of a Patent Disclosure or Licensing Statement.

For those SDOs that elect such a provision, careful attention should be paid to keeping all versions of the documents, as well as correspondence with the submitter, to ensure traceability of the changes.

3. Resubmission to the SDO

If the SDO rejects any Patent Disclosure or Licensing Statement pursuant to Section V.B.1 above, the SDO shall notify the Participant in writing of the reasons for such rejection. The Participant shall have a period of ____ days **[1]** *in which to submit a conforming Patent Disclosure or Licensing Statement, as applicable, without penalty.*

If the Participant fails [without good cause] to respond to the SDO or submit a conforming Patent Disclosure or Licensing Statement within such ____-day period, as determined in the discretion of the SDO, then the Participant shall be deemed to be in violation of the Policy and subject to the provisions of Section II.B.

[The Participant's response in the identified time period may also include a challenge to or interpretation of the rejection.]

1. This "cure period" should be sufficiently long to enable a Participant to cure an inadvertent breach of this obligation.

4. *Verification by the SDO*

Other than verification that all required fields have been completed as required by this Policy, the SDO will have no responsibility to verify any information contained in a Patent Disclosure or Licensing Statement (including whether or not the disclosed Claims are valid or enforceable, whether they cover the portions of the Standard asserted by the Patent Holder, or whether or not the Patent Holder has additional Claims that should have been disclosed).

Each Participant hereby acknowledges that the SDO has no responsibility or liability for any information contained in a Patent Disclosure or Licensing Statement.

Generally, SDOs do not assume responsibility to verify any information contained in a Patent Disclosure or Licensing Statement other than to ascertain whether the required fields, if any, have been completed as required by the Policy.

C. SDO NOTIFICATION AND DISCLAIMER

When an SDO receives a Patent Disclosure and/or a Licensing Statement, the text of the Standards Document [may/shall] include a note substantially as follows:

NOTE—Compliance with this standard may require a license under certain patent rights. Disclosures of patent rights that may be relevant to this Standard may be found at [www.location]. In addition, statements from identified Patent Holders regarding their intentions for licensing patent rights in connection with implementation of this standard may be viewed at [www.location].

The SDO takes no position with respect to the validity or enforceability of any patent and is not responsible for identifying patents or patent applications for which a license may be required to implement this standard.

This text is intended both to alert potential Implementers of the existence of potential Essential Claims, and to protect the SDO from legal claims by Implementers relating to the existence of such Essential Claims. Subsequent decisions to accept a Patent Holder's statements regarding the essentiality of Claims and to request a patent license are the responsibility of the Implementer.

D. POLICY GUIDELINES AND GUIDANCE

Some SDOs elect to produce a companion document to the Policy such as a "Guidelines to Implementation of [SDO] Patent Policy" or "Frequently Asked Questions regarding [SDO] Patent Policy." Such SDOs include ETSI, IEEE, ISO/IEC, ITU, TIA, and W3C; ANSI has also issued guidelines relating to its patent policy. Such documents may provide interpretive guidance relating to the Policy and its use. In addition, some SDOs use such documents to document the rationale and intent of the Policy or further binding interpretations (though the binding effect of such interpretations may be open to question to the extent that they are not expressly agreed to by Participants).

While such Guidelines may be helpful to users of the Policy, the SDO should carefully consider whether such Guidelines may be interpreted as providing additional, and possibly inconsistent, policy language.

Moreover, the SDO should be careful not to provide written guidance relating to the Policy or its interpretation without seeking legal advice. Informal advice that is provided by SDO personnel could, if not appropriately limited, be considered as binding and/or as part of the Policy.

Suggested legends to be included in any Guidelines or other companion documents to the Policy:

> *These Guidelines are intended to assist those that participate in the standards development process in understanding and implementing the SDO's Policy. By definition, Guidelines are suggestions and adherence is not essential for compliance with the SDO's Policy. Rather, the Guidelines are provided for purposes of effectively implementing and interpreting the SDO Policy.*
>
> *[These Guidelines supplement the SDO Policy and are not intended as a substitute for the Policy itself. In case of any disagreement, the SDO Policy takes precedence over these Guidelines.]*

Some SDOs prefer to clarify that the companion materials do not have the same status as Policy language, while other SDOs may prefer to use these materials to supplement their policies.

SECTION VII

Other Policy Provisions

A. EFFECT OF PARTICIPANT'S WITHDRAWAL FROM THE SDO

Section IV.C.6 above discusses the irrevocability of a Participant's existing Licensing Commitments after its withdrawal from the SDO. However, a Participant's withdrawal from an SDO may have other effects on its legal rights and the rights that it has granted to others. Below are policy clauses that address some of these other issues.

I. ***No Further Licensing Commitments.*** **Except as provided in [Section IV.E.1] above, a Participating Organization that withdraws from the SDO shall not be required to make any further Licensing Commitments following such withdrawal.**

II. ***Termination of Licensing Commitments Made to Withdrawing Participant.*** **Licensing Commitments made by Participants shall terminate with respect to any Participating Organization that withdraws from the SDO, effective upon such withdrawal [except to the extent that such Licensing Commitments are intended to cover all Implementers.]**

III. *Withdrawing Participant's Granted Licenses.* Nothing in this Policy, nor a Participant's withdrawal from the SDO, shall affect any license granted by the Participant. Any such license is a separate contractual arrangement between the parties thereto, and the Participant's withdrawal from the SDO shall not itself cause any termination of any such license unless expressly provided in such license.

Withdrawing Participant's Licensing Commitments. This provision is aimed at severing a withdrawing Participant's obligations for future activities it does not take part in. Note that this provision may interplay with other provisions, such as those relating to obligations that survive withdrawal described in Section IV.E.5.a.

Termination of Licensing Commitments Made to Withdrawing Participant. This clause should be used only if the beneficiaries of Licensing Commitments are limited to Participants in the SDO and the withdrawing Participant has no duty to make or continue to make any Licensing Commitment *vis-à-vis* the remaining Participants. In other words, the Licensing Commitments of the remaining Participants to the departing Participant should mirror the extent to which the departing Participant has either no or some scope of continuing commitments toward the remaining Participants. In any case, the withdrawing Participant should not be disadvantaged over other nonparticipants.

Withdrawing Participant's Granted Licenses. A Participant's withdrawal has no effect on granted licenses.

B. LICENSING COMMITMENTS AND INJUNCTIVE RELIEF

When a Patent Holder commits to grant licenses under its Essential Claims on RAND or RANDz terms, it promises to allow all manufacturers of standardized products to operate under those Essential Claims, subject to their acquiescence with those license terms. Numerous courts, governmental agencies, and commentators have concluded that making a Licensing Commitment should preclude a Patent Holder from seeking injunctive relief against an Implementer that is willing to accept such license terms.[1] A full analysis of this complex legal area is beyond the scope of this Guide.

This being said, some SDOs have sought to clarify whether Patent Holders that have made a Licensing Commitment may or may not seek injunctions and similar forms of exclusionary relief (such as exclusion orders issued by the U.S. International

---

1 *See*, e.g., Apple Inc. v. Motorola, Inc., 757 F.3d 1286, 1331–32 (Fed. Cir. 2014); Statement of the Fed. Trade Comm'n, Robert Bosch GmbH, FTC File No. 121-0081, at 2–3 (Nov. 26, 2012) (firm's attempt to obtain injunctive relief in the face of its FRAND commitment was inherently coercive and constituted an unfair method of competition in violation of Section 5 of the FTC Act); Decision and Order, Motorola Mobility LLC, FTC Docket No. C-4410, at 8 (July 23, 2013) (attempt to enjoin sales of products using its SEPs constituted an unfair method of competition in violation of Section 5 of the FTC Act); Letter from Renata B. Hesse, Acting Assistant Att'y Gen., U.S. Dep't of Justice, Antitrust Div., to Michael A. Lindsay, at 9 (Feb. 2, 2015) (it is "unlikely that a patent holder bound by a RAND commitment, even one that does not address explicitly the availability of injunctive relief, can secure an injunction (in addition to monetary damages) in an infringement action."); Joseph S. Miller, *Standard-Setting, Patents, and Access Lock-in: RAND Licensing and the Theory of the Firm*, 40 Ind. L. Rev. 351, 358 (2007) (the RAND promise creates an "irrevocable waiver of injunctive relief" that helps to prevent patent holdup); Douglas Lichtman, *Understanding the RAND Commitment*, 47 Hous. L. Rev. 1023, 1039–43 (2010) (injunctions should not apply in the RAND context); Suzanne Michel, *Bargaining For RAND Royalties In The Shadow Of Patent Remedies Law*, 77 Antitrust L.J. 889, 896–97 (2011) (allowing SEP holders to seek injunctive relief against standards implementers "can harm consumers and undermine the integrity of the standard-setting process"); Maurits Dolmans, *Standards For Standards*, 26 Fordham Intl. L.J. 163, 191–92 (2002) (seeking injunctive relief against a willing implementer would violate European competition law).

Trade Commission) against willing licensees.[2] The following provisions address this point:

> *For the avoidance of doubt* **[1]**, *a Participant that has made a Licensing Commitment with respect to Essential Claims shall not seek or threaten to obtain an injunction or other exclusionary order against an Implementer that has indicated its willingness* **[2]** *to enter into a license on the specified terms (RAND or RANDz) with respect to the practice of those Essential Claims [unless* **[3]** *the Implementer fails, within six months of initiation, to participate in, or to comply with the outcome of, an adjudication of the relevant license terms with the Patent Holders' Licensing Commitment by a court of competition jurisdiction or a recognized arbitral tribunal.]*

---

[2] *See*, e.g., IEEE Policy, *supra* note 11, Sec. 6.2 ("The Submitter of an Accepted LOA who has committed to make available a license for one or more Essential Patent Claims agrees that it shall neither seek nor seek to enforce a Prohibitive Order based on such Essential Patent Claim(s) in a jurisdiction unless [certain conditions occur]."); European Committee for Standardization & European Committee for Electrotechnical Standardization (CEN-CENELEC), Core Principles and Approaches for Licensing of Standard Essential Patents 9 (June 2019) ("Core Principle 1: A FRAND SEP holder must not threaten, seek or enforce an injunction (or similar de facto exclusion processes) except in exceptional circumstances and only where FRAND compensation cannot be addressed via adjudication, e.g., lack of jurisdiction or bankruptcy. Parties should seek to negotiate FRAND terms without any unfair 'hold up' leverage associated with injunctions or other de facto market exclusion processes."); European Association of Automotive Suppliers (CLEPA), Standard Essential Patents (SEPs) and Fair, Reasonable & Non-Discriminatory (FRAND) Licensing 3–4 (2021) ("[i]f parties disagree regarding SEP licenses, those disputes should be resolved by the national courts . . . without the threat of market exclusion, especially where . . . the licensee is willing to pay an established FRAND rate.")

1. Note that this clause exists for clarification purposes and may be duplicative of protections already granted under applicable national law.
2. The "willingness" of an Implementer to enter into a license on RAND or RANDz terms may be difficult to determine, and most SDOs will be reluctant to make such determinations. However, an SDO may wish to include language in its policy indicating what may or may not indicate whether a potential licensee is willing. For example, the following indicia of unwillingness have been suggested in various contexts:

- The prospective licensee has stated that it refuses to accept a license on RAND terms;
- The prospective licensee has failed to enter into good faith licensing negotiations after some reasonable period of time (e.g., 180 days);
- The prospective licensee lacks the resources to pay a RAND royalty and has demonstrated no ability to do so.

By the same token, an SDO may wish to describe certain actions that would not generally characterize a potential licensee as unwilling:

- The prospective licensee questions whether the Patent Holder has complied with its obligation to offer RAND terms;
- The prospective licensee challenges the validity, essentiality, and/or or enforceability of some or all proffered Essential Claims;
- The prospective licensee requests legitimate information from the Patent Holder concerning patent claim coverage, comparable license agreements and the like in order to better inform itself regarding the proffered terms of a

license and assess the Patent Holder's compliance with its RAND obligation.

3. This optional clause permits the Patent Holder to seek injunctive relief if the Implementer fails to participate in a judicial or arbitration determination of relevant RAND terms within six months of the initiation of such a determination proceeding, or if the Implementer fails to abide by the outcome of such a proceeding.[3]

C. DISPUTE RESOLUTION

Like other commercial agreements, SDO patent policies may specify how disputes will be resolved among Participants in lieu of litigation. A few SDOs require that such disputes be resolved by binding arbitration,[4] either by an independent arbitral tribunal such as the International Chamber of Commerce (ICC) or the American Arbitration Association (AAA),[5] or via internal SDO dispute adjudication mechanisms.[6] While there are many ways to implement such provisions, a simple clause follows:

Each Participant hereby agrees, on its behalf and on behalf of its Affiliates, that all disputes with any other

---

[3] Such a provision is included in the IEEE Policy, *supra* note 11, as well as the Consent Decrees issued by the Federal Trade Commission in Robert Bosch and Google/Motorola, *supra* note 48.

[4] For a discussion, *see* Jorge L. Contreras & David Newman, *Developing a Framework for Arbitrating Standards-Essential Patent Disputes*, 2014 J. Dispute Resol. 23 (2014).

[5] *See* THE DVB PROJECT, Memorandum of Understanding of the DVB Project, Article 14: Intellectual Property Rights (2014), https://www.dvb.org/resources/public/documents_site/dvb_mou.pdf; BLU-RAY DISC ASSOCIATION, By-laws, Amended & Restated Bylaws of Blu-Ray Disc Association, cl. 16, (Oct. 1, 2010), http://www.blu-raydisc.com/Assets/Downloadablefile/BDA_Bylaws_%28v2.0%29-18618.pdf.

[6] *See* VITA Policy, *supra* note 14, Sec. 10.5.

> *Participant regarding the interpretation or enforcement of this Policy or any Patent Disclosure, Licensing Commitment, or Licensing Statement made hereunder shall be finally resolved and settled under the [RULES] of [TRIBUNAL] by [three] arbitrators appointed in accordance with such Rules. Arbitration shall take place in [LOCATION]. The language of the arbitral proceedings shall be the English language unless agreed otherwise between the Participants, and each Participant shall bear its own costs and expenses of arbitration. [For the avoidance of doubt, this clause does not apply to disputes arising under license agreements that are entered into by Participants.]*

It should be recognized, however, that requiring parties to waive their right of access to the national courts could be controversial and may deter SDO participation. In addition, alternative dispute resolution mechanisms may not support similar due process, discovery, or substantive claims or defenses, and may be confidential and non-precedential. For these reasons, such processes could be considered by some participants as less desirable than court processes.

D. CHOICE OF LAW

An SDO patent policy is a legal document and, as such, may need to be interpreted by an adjudicator, whether a court or arbitrator, in the event of a disagreement among Participants. When such interpretation occurs, the adjudicator may need to apply legal principles of interpretation, procedure, or substantive law. Those principles will be found in the national law of some countries. If the policy itself does not specify which national laws should be used in such interpretation, then the adjudicator may choose an appropriate set of laws—often those of its own jurisdiction. However, in such a vacuum, there is little to prevent adjudicators in different jurisdictions each from applying their own local laws, resulting in a cacophony of interpretative guidance for the same policy. To avoid these problems, many SDOs specify the national laws that will govern their policies.

It should also be noted and considered that patent laws are subject to the laws of individual countries. The ways in which reasonable patent royalties are considered in one jurisdiction may not accord with the approaches taken in another. As such, it may not be appropriate to have one court (e.g., in the chosen jurisdiction) seek to apply its own remedial approaches to determine how the reasonable rates (or validity, or infringement) for national patents of another jurisdiction might be evaluated. This national character of patent law can provide significant difficulties in assessing patent issues, and this may not be addressed by a contractual choice of law clause.

Choosing the law to govern an SDO policy is not always straightforward. Many SDOs reflexively choose the laws of their jurisdiction of incorporation, as these laws will in any event apply to many issues of membership, governance, and financial solvency. However, given the international scope of many SDOs, it is not necessary that the laws of the jurisdiction of incorporation govern their patent policies. In fact, such choices have occasionally caused some confusion. For example, when it was formed in the late 1980s, ETSI was incorporated in France and, thus, specified that the laws of France would govern its patent policy.[7] However, relatively few ETSI participants are based in France, speak the French language, or have familiarity with the doctrines of French law. As a result, ETSI operates largely on international consensus understandings of various principles of standard-setting and competition law, with French law invoked only in litigation between members. And when such

7 ETSI Policy, *supra* note 11, Sec. 12.

litigation occurs, dueling French law experts often produce different interpretations of ETSI's requirements. As a result, courts in other countries attempting to apply French law tend to take shortcuts and assume that French law principles are identical to those of their own countries.[8]

Nevertheless, selecting some national law to govern an SDO policy is better than selecting none at all. The following policy language can be used to do so:

> *The interpretation and enforcement of this Policy, and the Participants' obligations and rights hereunder, shall be interpreted in accordance with the laws of [______________] without reference to its principles of conflict of laws.*

---

8 For example, in Apple v. Motorola, a U.S. federal district judge sitting in Wisconsin was required to determine whether Motorola violated its contractual obligation to offer a FRAND license to Apple. In assessing Motorola's obligation under ETSI's patent policy, the judge reviewed a French law professor's affidavit submitted on behalf of one party and the other party's excerpt from an English-language treatise on French contract law. She concludes that French law "requires the same general elements" for contract formation as Wisconsin law, and makes little effort to apply French statutory law to the case. 886 F. Supp. 2d 1061, 1082 (W.D. Wis. 2012).

Appendix A

Disclosure and Licensing Templates to Accompany SDO Patent Policies

When developing a patent policy, an SDO should decide whether (a) to require the use of a standardized template or form for all patent disclosures and/or licensing statements, (b) to offer a template, but not to require its use so long as the Participant complies with the requirements of the patent policy, or (c) to offer no template at all. This last choice can be staff-intensive and may not lead to consistent disclosure statements or licensing commitments to the SDO.

When templates (whether required or optional) are being developed to accompany a patent policy, several factors should be taken into consideration. One of the most important factors is ensuring consistency of the form with the patent policy. The viewpoint of those who will interface with the form in one way or another (submitter, SDO staff, general viewers of the data of the form) should be a significant consideration, which may influence the complexity of the form and the intended display and/or use of data contained in the form. Enforcement and legal validity should also be considered. Updating information (such as contact information, patent application status, etc.) contained on the form or in a form-driven database is another consideration. In addition, companies (including the intellectual property they own), are merged, divested, sold, and otherwise transferred over time. Thus, patent disclosure information needs to be maintained over time to handle different circumstances.

Consistency of the form with the patent policy

The SDO should carefully develop text for the forms that corresponds to the exact wording in the patent policy. Attention should be paid so as to not introduce new definitions or concepts that are not reflected in the patent policy or that may be additive or inconsistent from those contained in the policy. However, it is not advised to have too much language from the patent policy repeated throughout the form but rather, where appropriate to increase understanding, insert cross-references to the pertinent portions of the patent policy within the text of the form. For example, a cross-reference might state:

> *In accordance with clause xxx of the SDO [policy/bylaws/procedures], the company's licensing position is:*

Also important for the user of the form is to have some kind of notation within the form indicating that the terms and definitions are set forth in the patent policy and provide a link to the available key related documents and their effective date. An example of such language is:

> *The SDO patent policy and the procedures used to execute that policy are documented in the SDO xxxx [policy/bylaw/procedures], available at xxxxxx [Web link or staff contact]. The terms and definitions in the SDO [policy/bylaws/procedures] in effect as of the date of this [form name] are incorporated herein.*

Often when designing a draft form for a draft policy, the SDO will discover areas not completely addressed or defined in the patent policy. The SDO can then use the discrepancies discovered to further improve the wording of the policy. The activity of trying to "implement" the proposed policy via the proposed forms may yield gaps in the proposed policy.

Furthermore, consideration should be given to the designation of the form within the SDO policy or operating procedures. Namely, if the SDO has a hierarchy of documents, it should be ensured that any change made to the patent policy will also result in corresponding changes to the forms. If the SDO policy permits changes to the forms without necessarily updating the patent policy, the resulting form may contain explicit or implicit requirements that are not contained in the policy. This is sometimes referred to as "form creep." There should not be "requirements" contained in the forms that are not reflected in the policy. Every effort should be made to keep all related documents to the patent policy aligned, including periodic scheduled verification of that alignment.

Complexity of the form

Generally, the more concise the form is, the easier it is for the Participant to complete. Careful consideration should be given to which fields must be completed within the form and to the sequence in which the required information is requested. However, a concise form that does not elicit sufficient information or detail would not be desirable.

Recognizing that contact points for a patent holder may change over time, consideration should be given to having a Title or Patent Department listed as the prime contact point, with a secondary field to list a particular person submitting that particular patent disclosure statement. The individual submitting the form should be the contact point for further information with regard to licensing of that patent.

Intended display and/or use of data contained in forms

Some SDOs post all Patent Disclosures received online. Sometimes they are multiply indexed, by company name and also by document number or standard number to which the patent disclosure statement applies. Some SDOs elect to make patent disclosure statements and/or licensing statements available only upon written request. The actual statements are not posted on the SDO website. This option may be selected by an SDO with limited resources, or by an SDO that seldom receives statements from patent holders, or when outside requests for such statements are rare.

It has become increasingly common for an SDO to use its website to post information from forms received. When considering the choice of format to display the information received in forms associated with the patent policy, the SDO must consider what format it will use for making forms available, and what data will be displayed on the SDO website. For example, it may want to consider in what manner the selected data from the forms will be displayed on the SDO website, that is, a searchable format, query features, key information displayed, a database index of the patent disclosure statements, etc.

Some SDOs elect to scan the actual Patent Disclosure in whatever format it is received and subsequently post the scanned version to the SDO website. The advantage of scanning the forms as received and posting on the SDO website by some key attribute (such as name of the standard or name of submitter) is that SDO staff may not have to re-enter information from the forms. This can minimize induced transcription errors that could expose the SDO to liability in a patent or patent policy dispute. However, depending on the design of the SDO website, SDO staff still may be required to enter pieces of key data from the scanned form into some kind of web-based tool to provide a summary report for parties who wish to have some sort of search engine to identify which scanned forms are of interest. The disadvantage of scanning forms is that there may be increased data entry by SDO staff since there is no web-based tool to discern data from the form.

Patent Disclosures can also be made available in a web-hosted static form such as Adobe Acrobat PDF format or other image format protocol, where the Participant can enter data only in certain fields. Providing such a format allows the SDO staff to have a reasonable level of confidence that the original data submitted is accurate, and to have a web-based tool behind the scenes to discern selected data. This in turn may minimize data entry and date entry errors by SDO staff but still requires SDO staff oversight.

Some SDOs elect to provide an editable word-processing version of the form that is made available to the Participants. A Participant can enter the data and email the completed form to the appropriate staff. Permitting an editable format allows the Participant more flexibility in preparing forms; however, the SDO staff must ensure that the submitted form retains the information as submitted and was not unintentionally manipulated or changed when the document was viewed or scanned.

SDOs can design a web-based form which the Participant completes online; the participant then receives a summary of the information submitted via the SDO web tool. The submitted information is used to populate an SDO web-based database and the information is displayed on the SDO website. It is prudent for SDO staff to screen information contained in the form to ensure compliance with the policy before the data is displayed online.

The advantage of a well-designed web-based form is that it should minimize (i) SDO staff data entry, (ii) chance for transcription errors, and (iii) staff oversight. Furthermore, the data can be parsed and a database can be designed so that viewers of the SDO patent disclosure statements and/or licensing statements can view and search the data. The disadvantage is that a certain degree of expertise and effort must be invested to design a web-based form and database, and this option may not be possible for an SDO with limited resources.

If the SDO's patent policy changes and/or the forms change, it may be helpful to have a clear way to indicate under which patent policy any submitted form or statement was made.

Finally, SDOs should consider including disclaimer language on any website reflecting information received from patent holders. Such a disclaimer could include statements to the effect that the SDO is not taking any position as to whether (a) the disclosed patents are valid or essential, (b) that any information reflected is current, accurate, and/or complete, and (c) any disclosure satisfies the requirements of the SDO's patent policy.

Appendix B

Sample Licensing Agreements for Standards-Essential Patents

1. Patent License Agreement (FRAND) developed by the UK High Court (Patents) in *Unwired Planet v. Huawei* and appended to its decision at [2017] EWHC 1304 (Pat) (7 Jun 2017).
2. Patent License Agreement Terms from Amended Final Judgment and Injunction in *TCL Communication Technology Holdings, Ltd v. Telefonaktiebolaget LM Ericsson*, Case No. 8:14-CV-00341 JVS-DFMx (C.D. Cal., Dec. 22, 2017)

Appendix B1

Patent License Agreement

by and between

Unwired Planet Limited Liability Company Unwired Planet International Limited

and

Huawei Technologies Co., Ltd.

Huawei Technologies (UK) Co., Ltd.

This agreement (hereinafter referred to as the "**Agreement**") is made on this day of ______________________("**Date**") by and between: Unwired Planet Limited Liability Company, a corporation organized and existing under the laws of the State of Nevada, having its principal place of business at 7160 Dallas Parkway, Suite 250, Plano, Texas, 75024, USA ("UPLLC") and Unwired Planet International Limited, a corporation organized and existing under the laws of Ireland, having its principal place of business at The Hyde Building, Unit 32, The Park Carrickmines, Dublin 18, 662898 Ireland ("UPIL") (together hereinafter referred to as "**Unwired Planet**" or "**Licensor**"); and Huawei Technologies Co., Ltd., a corporation organized and existing under the laws of China, having its headquarters at Huawei Industrial Base, Bantian, Longgang District, Shenzhen, 518129, China, ("**Huawei China**") and Huawei Technologies (UK) Co., Ltd., a corporation organized and existing under the laws of the United Kingdom, having its principle place of business at 300 South Oak Way, Green Park, Reading, Berkshire RG2 6UF ("**Huawei UK**") (together hereinafter referred to as "**Huawei**" or "**Licensee**").

WHEREAS Unwired Planet owns, controls or is otherwise entitled to grant rights under certain patents and patent applications relating to Licensed Products (as hereinafter defined) and Huawei manufactures, sells and distributes certain Licensed Products; and

WHEREAS Unwired Planet is willing to grant a license and Huawei is willing to obtain such a license under the Licensed Patents on the terms and conditions set forth in this Agreement.

Where appropriate, Unwired Planet and Huawei shall hereinafter be referred to collectively as "**Parties**" and individually as "**Party**" or as Licensor, Licensee, Unwired Planet and Huawei as the context may require.

NOW THEREFORE in consideration of the premises and mutual covenants herein contained, the Parties hereby agree as follows:

1. Definitions

1.1. The following capitalized terms used in this Agreement shall have the respective meanings ascribed to them below in this Section unless otherwise expressly defined in this Agreement (such definitions shall be equally applicable to both the singular and plural forms of the defined terms). The words "hereof," "herein" and "hereunder" and words of like import when used in this Agreement shall refer to this Agreement as a whole and not to any particular provision of this Agreement, and Section references are to this Agreement unless otherwise specified. For the purpose of the construction and interpretation of this Agreement, the word "including" (and variations thereof such as "include" and "includes") and the phrase "such as" will not be deemed to be terms of limitation, but rather will be deemed to be followed by the words "without limitation".

1.2. "Affiliate" of a Party or Third Party means an Entity that at any time controls, is controlled by, or is under common control with such Party or Third Party. Such Entities shall only be deemed to be Affiliates hereunder for as long as such control exists. Control, in this context, (hereinafter referred as "Control") exists where one entity owns more than 50% whether directly or indirectly of the Voting Power or, if the Entity in question does not have outstanding voting shares or securities, more than 50% of the equity interest in such Entity.

1.3. "Combination" means two (2) or more items comprising part of a combination of products, software and/or services being sold by

Licensee or its Affiliates, as part of the same transaction or a series of linked transactions which is comprised of, at a minimum, an End User Device or a piece of Infrastructure Equipment.

1.4. "Effective Date" means 1 January 2013.

1.5. "End User Device" means a complete wireless communication device (including but not limited to mobile phones, PCs, laptops, tablets, hotspots, access points, routers, home gateways, data cards, which is ready for use (even if a battery, SIM card, or the like needs to be added for use) as Sold by Licensee or its Affiliates, and which can be directly used by an end user for 2G, 3G, and/or 4G cellular communications. End User Devices may be capable of operating according to more than one cellular standard mode (for example, 2G, 3G, 4G), but at least one of the modes must be 2G, 3G, or 4G. End-User Device does not mean, without limitation, subassemblies or parts of products such as but not limited to Intermediate Products, other than as sold already incorporated into an End User Device.

1.6. "Entity" means any individual, firm, company, corporation or other corporate body or legal entity (wherever and however incorporated or established), government, state, agency or agency of a state, local or municipal authority or government body or any joint venture, association or partnership (whether or not having a separate legal personality).

1.7. "Have Made" means the right to have a Third Party make Licensed Products for the use and benefit of the Licensee and its Affiliates provided all of the following conditions are fulfilled:

(a) the Licensed Products are made under contract by a Third Party manufacturer for Licensee or its Affiliates and are supplied by such Third Party manufacturer solely to Licensee or its Affiliates (or directly to their customers on behalf of Licensee or its Affiliates) and to no other Third Party; and

(b) such Licensed Products are not re-Sold back to, or on behalf of, such Third Party manufacturers or its Affiliates.

1.8. "Licensed Products" means End User Devices and Infrastructure Equipment that are: (a) branded with a brand owned by or licensed to Licensee and/or its Affiliates, or co-branded with a brand owned by or licensed to Licensee and/or its Affiliates with that of a brand owned by or licensed to one or more Third Parties, or (b) manufactured by, or for (under Have Made rights), Licensee and/or its Affiliates and sold to Third Parties (e.g., Vodafone, Carphone Warehouse, distributors and retailers) as Licensee's, or Licensee's Affiliates' own products, or to Carriers for use and/or sale by Carrier under its own brand ("Carrier" being Vodafone, EE, O2, MVNOs (mobile virtual network operators), and the like that offer cellular service to customers). Licensed Products shall not include Intermediate Products.

1.9. "Infrastructure Equipment" means radio access network elements (such as base stations (including pico base stations, and femto base stations, NodeB, and eNodeB), base station controllers and radio network controllers) including software necessary to operate and integral to any of the foregoing, regardless of whether the software is provided with the hardware or sold separately. This definition of Infrastructure Equipment does not include any End User Devices, intermediate products or subassemblies, such as but not limited to Intermediate Products, other than those that are incorporated in the complete and ready to use Infrastructure Equipment as Sold by the respective Party (and/or their Affiliates as applicable).

1.10. "Infrastructure Revenue" means all revenues derived from the Sales of licensed Infrastructure Equipment. For the avoidance of doubt, Infrastructure Revenue shall not include any revenues derived from maintenance or operation of the Infrastructure Equipment.

1.11. "Intermediate Products" means any item of equipment, including, for example, a sub-system, sub-assembly or component, in software, hardware and/or firmware form, which is sold, licensed, or supplied, or intended to be sold, licensed or supplied by Licensee or its Affiliates to a Third Party for use as an intermediate product in an end-use item, because it requires additional industrial, manufacturing or assembly processes before being used or sold as an end-use item, and is intended for incorporation into a larger item of end-use equipment or product. Examples of Intermediate Products include ASICs, chipsets, printed circuit boards, integrated circuits (ICs), processors, multi-core processors, multi-chip modules, multi-chip packages, embedded modules, core engines and M2M modules.

1.12. "Patent" shall mean patent claims (including claims of licensable patent applications, whether or not divisionals, continuations, continuations-in-part, reissues, renewals, and extensions therefore and any counterparts claiming priority therefrom), and like statutory rights other than design patents.

1.13. "Licensed Patents" shall mean all Patents that were at any time owned, controlled or licensable by Licensor, Unwired Planet LLC, UP Optis Holding LLC, UP IP Management, Inc. and / or their Subsidiaries during the Term as to which it is, or claimed, declared or otherwise asserted by the owner to be, not possible, on technical grounds taking into account normal technical practice and the state of the art generally available at the time of adoption or publication of the relevant Standards, to make, sell, offer for sale, lease or otherwise dispose of and import, repair, use or operate equipment or methods which comply with the relevant Standards, without infringing such Patents, as determined by the applicable law of the country to which the Patents pertain and shall further include patents in litigation as listed in Annex B; provided, however, that (a) any Patents assigned by the Licensor to Lenovo Group pursuant to the Patent Purchase Agreement dated 20 March 2014 and (b) Patents owned or controlled by Licensor that were owned or controlled by Samsung or its Affiliates prior to being owned or controlled by Licensor, as listed in Annex C, shall not be considered Licensed Patents under this Agreement. For the purpose of this definition, "Subsidiary" means an Entity that at any time is Controlled by a Party.

1.14. "Selling Price" shall mean with respect to each Licensed Product Sold by Licensee or any of its Affiliates, one of the following, whichever is applicable:

1.15. When Sold to an Unrelated Buyer, the Selling Price will be a) the selling price charged by Licensee or its Affiliate for such Licensed Product, or b) if the Licensed Product has been Sold as part of a Sale including other type of products (i.e. not only Licensed Products) and the selling price in question is an amount lower than the Average Selling Price (as defined below), then such Average Selling

Price shall be used for the Selling Price. For the purpose of this Agreement, "Average Selling Price" shall mean the average selling price, charged by Licensee and its Affiliates for equivalent or substantially equivalent Licensed Products that have not been Sold as part of a Sale including other type of Licensee's products, during the same or most recent calendar quarter in which Licensee and its Affiliates Sold substantial quantities of such equivalent Licensed Products (or if substantial quantities of such equivalent Licensed Products have not been Sold during any such calendar quarter, substantial quantities of substantially equivalent Licensee Products that have not been Sold as part of a Sale including other type of Licensee's products,) to Unrelated Buyers, or if substantial quantities of such equivalent or substantially equivalent Licensed Products have not been Sold to an Unrelated Buyer by Licensee and its Affiliates in accordance with above during any such calendar quarter, the costs to Licensee or its Affiliate, as the case may be, to produce (or otherwise acquire) such Licensed Products plus twenty percent (20%) of such costs; or

1.16. With respect to Sales to a Related Buyer, the Selling Price for each such Licensed Product shall be a) the selling price charged by the final vendee Related Buyer of such Licensed Product to an Unrelated Buyer for such Licensed Product, or b) if the Licensed Product has been Sold as part of a Sale including other type of Licensee's products (i.e. not only Licensed Products) and selling price in question is lower than the Average Selling Price, then such Average Selling Price shall be used instead, or, if no further Sale of such Licensee Product is made by the Related Buyer to an Unrelated Buyer, then the Selling Price for each such Licensed Product shall be the Average Selling Price for the Licensee Product.

1.17. "Net Selling Price" shall mean the Selling Price of each Licensed Product that is not Infrastructure Equipment, in the form in which it is Sold; whether or not assembled and without excluding therefrom any components or subassemblies thereof. In determining the Selling Price import tax, export tax and other sales taxes and/or customs duties levied or imposed directly upon the Sale of such Licensed Products shall be excluded, and a four percent (4%) of the actual invoiced amount shall be deducted representing usual trade discount, packing costs, insurance and transportation costs. For the avoidance of doubt, any price for after sales support, which is either specified on the invoice or the contract for such Huawei Products Sold, shall not be included in the Net Selling Price definition.

1.18. "Related Buyer" means an Entity that is not an Unrelated Buyer or an Affiliate.

1.19. "Unrelated Buyer" means a person or Entity that does not control Licensee or its Affiliates, is not controlled by Licensee or its Affiliates, and is not in common control with Licensee or its Affiliates; and the term "control" for the purposes of this definition means the direct or indirect ownership or control of more than a thirty percent (30%) equity interest or more than thirty percent (30%) of the Voting Power.

1.20. "Sale", "Sell" or "Sold" or any similar variation of such term, means the delivery of Licensed Products in the Territory to a Third Party for compensation, if any, including lease, rent or similar transaction, or the putting into use of the Licensed Products by the Licensee and/or its Affiliates for any purpose other than routine testing, quality control or certification– with a Sale being deemed to have occurred upon invoicing or such putting into use in the Territory, whichever shall first occur. For the avoidance of doubt, any delivery of samples, repairs or replacements of End User Devices in the Territory, regardless of the basis for compensation, shall not be considered to be a "Sale".

1.21. "Standards" means the agreed protocols by 3GPP, ETSI, ARIB and/or other relevant telecommunications standards setting bodies that are applicable to the 2G, 3G and/or 4G telecommunication standards (as defined herein) including any updates, modifications and extensions of such protocols. For clarity, Standard shall not include 5G telecommunications standards.

1.22. "Term" means the term of this Agreement which shall be from and including the Effective Date through and ending on 31 December 2020, unless earlier terminated in accordance with the provisions herein.

1.23. "Territory" means world-wide.

1.24. "Third Party" means any Entity that is not a Party or an Affiliate of a Party.

1.25. "Voting Power" means the right to exercise voting power with respect to the election of directors or similar managing authority of an Entity (whether through direct or indirect beneficial ownership of shares or securities of such Entity or otherwise).

1.26. "2G" means Global System for Mobile Communications (GSM) and General Packet Radio System (GPRS) including Enhanced GPRS (E-GPRS or "EDGE") standard specifications released or published by 3GPP and/or relevant local standardization bodies such as ETSI, TIA, T1P1, ARIB, TTC and CCSA, irrespective of the transmission medium, frequency band or duplexing scheme, at the time of the Effective Date as well as updates in respect of such standard specifications during the Term.

1.27. "3G" means UTRA (FDD mode (including but not limited to WCDMA) and TDD mode), including HSPA and UMTS core network standard specifications, however excluding TD-SCDMA standard specifications, released or published by 3GPP and/or relevant local standardization bodies such as ETSI, TIA, T1P1, ARIB, TTC and CCSA, irrespective of the transmission medium, frequency band or duplexing scheme, at the time of the Effective Date, as well as any updates in respect of such standard specifications during the Term.

1.28. "4G" means E-UTRA (FDD mode and TDD mode (including but not limited to LTE, TD-LTE and LTE-SAE)), standard specifications released or published by 3GPP and/or relevant local standardization bodies such as but not limited to ETSI, TIA, T1P1, ARIB, TTC and CCSA, irrespective of the transmission medium, frequency band or duplexing scheme, at the time of the Effective Date, including Release 8 and LTE-Advanced, as well as any updates in respect of such standard specifications during the Term.

1.29. "Major Market" shall mean, in respect of 2G or 3G Standards, a country in which there are two (2) or more Licensed Patents (but excluding China), and in respect of 4G, a country in which there are three (3) or more Licensed Patents (but excluding China). At the Date, the countries in the following table are Major Markets (referred to in the table as "MM") for the Standards indicated:

MM all standards	MM 4G and 3G	MM 4G only	MM 3G only
France	Canada	Ireland	Argentina
Germany	Italy	Netherlands	Australia
India	Spain	New Zealand	South Korea
Japan	Taiwan	Switzerland	
UK			
US			

1.30. "Other Markets" shall mean any country which is not a Major Market, but excluding China.

2. Grant of License

2.1. Subject to payment of royalties in accordance with Section 4 of this Agreement, Licensor, on behalf of itself, its Affiliates, and their respective predecessors, successors and assigns, hereby grants (and shall procure that its Affiliates grant) Licensee a non-exclusive, non-transferable, royalty bearing license under the Licensed Patents in the Territory during the Term to:

2.1.1. possess, use, import, Sell and offer for Sale, lease, furnish, transfer or otherwise dispose or supply of any and all Licensed Products;

2.1.2. make, import, use and maintain machines, tools, materials and all other instrumentalities and to practice methods, processes and services for the development, manufacture, testing and repair of Licensed Products; and

2.1.3. make, manufacture and Have Made Licensed Products.

2.2. For the express avoidance of doubt, the rights provided at Section 2.1 above do not include any rights or licenses:

2.2.1. to sell or offer to sell Intermediate Products except for the purpose of repair and maintenance of any Licensed Product;

2.2.2. under any Patent other than the Licensed Patents;

2.2.3. to manufacture or sell products that are based on a Third Party design and are sold by Licensee or its Affiliates to or on behalf of such Third Party as the Third Party's own product and not a Licensed Product. Save always that this Section 2.2.3 shall not apply to Carriers, whether those Licensed Products are made to the Carrier's specifications or not, or whether those Licensed Products carry a Licensee brand or not.

2.3. Subject to the payment according to Section 4 of this Agreement, the licenses granted herein by Licensor shall include the right of Licensee to grant sublicenses under Section 2.1 herein, without further payment to Licensor for such right of sublicense, to its Affiliates in the Territory during the Term. No such sublicense shall be broader in any respect than the license held at that time by Licensee. The right to grant sublicenses to an Affiliate shall apply only during the time period when such Affiliate meets the requirements of an Affiliate. Licensee acknowledges that any sublicensed Affiliate will be bound in all respects to all of the obligations contained in this Agreement and Licensee shall be responsible for compliance by its sublicensed Affiliates with such obligations. Licensee shall be primarily responsible for the compensations set forth in Section 4 below for the activities of any sublicensed Affiliate. Any sublicense granted in accordance with this Section 2.3 shall immediately terminate if an Affiliate ceases to be an Affiliate of Licensee and otherwise upon termination of this Agreement

2.4. For the avoidance of doubt, the license granted by Licensor and its Affiliates to Licensee herein shall convey to any direct or indirect customer of Licensee without additional compensation to Licensor with respect to any Licensed Product Sold by Licensee to such customer (whether or not as part of a Combination) the benefit under the license herein.

2.5. There may be countries in which Licensee and/or its Affiliates may have, as a consequence of this Agreement, rights against infringers of the Licensed Patents. Licensee hereby waives, and shall procure the waiver from its Affiliates, of any such right Licensee or any

Affiliate may have by reason of any Third Party's infringement of any such Licensed Patents.

2.6. All rights not expressly granted herein by Licensor are hereby expressly reserved. Nothing in this Agreement shall be construed as conveying whether explicitly, by principles of implied license, or otherwise, any license rights not explicitly granted herein. Furthermore, nothing in this Agreement shall be construed as conveying whether explicitly, by principles of implied license, or otherwise, any rights to any Third Party user or purchaser of the Licensed Products, under any Licensed Patent covering any combination of the Licensed Products with any other product (not licensed hereunder) where the patent claim applies specifically to the combination and not to the Licensed Product alone, except to the extent that (i) such claim would have been infringed (either directly, by inducement, or by contributory infringement) by Licensed Products or its process in the absence of such combination, that (ii) such claim would have been infringed by such combination where a Licensed Product is an essential element of such infringement, or that (iii) such claim would be subject to patent exhaustion based on sales of Licensed Products.

3. Release

3.1. Subject to Licensee's payment of it and its Affiliates unlicensed past activities (activities between the Effective Date and the Date) in the form of royalties as set out at Section 4, Licensor, on behalf of itself, its Affiliates, and its and their respective predecessors, successors and assigns, (the "Licensor Releasing Parties"), forever releases and discharges Licensee and its Affiliates, their predecessors, successors and assigns, their respective directors, officers, managers, their contract manufacturers, distributors, resellers, and their direct and indirect customers (the "Licensee Released Parties"), from any and all claims, counterclaims, causes of action (regardless of whether they are now known or unknown, suspected or unsuspected) that the Licensor Releasing Parties may have on account of the Licensee Released Parties' acts of infringement or alleged infringement by reason of having done any of the acts specified in Sections 2.1.1-2.1.3 inclusive until (but not including) the Date, provided always that such act would be licensed under this Agreement had it occurred subsequent to the Date.

4. Payment

4.1. In consideration of the license and release granted herein, Licensee shall pay to Licensor the following amounts (referred to in this Section 4 as either "royalty sum", "royalties" or royalty") in respect of Licensee's and its Affiliates' activities in the Territory during the Term:

4.2. For End User Devices:

4.2.1. 0.064% of the Net Selling Price for each End User Device compliant with 2G only that is Sold in Major Markets and 0.016% of the Net Selling Price for each End User Device compliant with 2G only that is Sold in Other Markets or China;

4.2.2. 0.032% of the Net Selling Price for each End User Device compliant with at least 3G but not 4G that is Sold in Major Markets and 0.016% of the Net Selling Price for each End User Device compliant with at least 3G but not 4G that is Sold in Other Markets or China;

4.2.3. 0.052% of the Net Selling Price for each End User Device compliant with at least 4G that is Sold in Major Markets and 0.026% of the Net Selling Price for each End User Device compliant with at least 4G that is Sold in Other Markets or China.

4.3. For Infrastructure Equipment:

4.3.1. 0.064% of Infrastructure Revenue for Infrastructure Equipment compliant with 2G that is Sold in Major Markets and 0.032% of the Infrastructure Revenue for Infrastructure Equipment compliant with 2G that is Sold in Other Markets or China;

4.3.2. 0.016% of Infrastructure Revenue for Infrastructure Equipment compliant with 3G that is Sold in Major Markets and 0.004% of the Infrastructure Revenue for Infrastructure Equipment compliant with 3G that is Sold in Other Markets or China;

4.3.3. 0.051% of Infrastructure Revenue for Infrastructure Equipment compliant with 4G that is Sold in Major Markets and 0.026% of the Infrastructure Revenue for Infrastructure Equipment compliant with 4G that is Sold in Other Markets or China.

The Parties acknowledge and agree that to the extent the Infrastructure Equipment is only compliant with one Standard individually (for example 4G), this clause shall not be interpreted as an admission that Licensee shall pay for the other Standards (for example 2G and/or 3G) and no separate payment shall be due for the other standard(s); nor shall this clause be interpreted as Licensee's admission that it has Infrastructure Equipment operating in more than one Standard (i.e. a combination of 2G and 3G).

4.4. Adjustments to the list of Major Markets in Section 1.27 will be done on an annual basis. Any Licensed Patent in a country which is determined by a relevant court to be invalid or not essential would cease to count as a Licensed Patent in that country. Further, if additional Licensed Patents are added in a country appropriate adjustments shall be made.

4.5. In the event that Licensee purchases components that carry a license ("**Pass Through License**") under any of the Licensed Patents ("**Prior Licensed Patents**"); and such components are used by Licensee in Licensed Products in a manner licensed under such Pass Through License, then, for the term of such Pass Through License, Licensee shall have no license under this Agreement to such Prior Licensed Patents and will have no royalty obligation, under this Agreement, with regard to such Prior Licensed Patents to the extent licensed under such Pass Through License. For the avoidance of doubt, if a patent applies to both 3G and 4G Standards and is licensed under the Pass Through License for 3G but not 4G, then the patent would be a Prior License Patent for 3G and remain a Licensed Patent for 4G. In the event of a dispute, Section 10 of this Agreement shall apply.

4.6. Licensee shall, on behalf of itself and its Affiliates, pay to Licensor the royalties as specified in Sections 4.2 and 4.3 above no later than forty-five (45) days from and including the day the report is due according to Section 4.8 below. Licensor shall issue written invoices, corresponding to the reported amounts and applicable report period, no later than thirty (30) days from and including the payment due date provided in this Section 4.4. Any termination of this Agreement shall not preclude the right of Licensor to be paid all royalties due and accruing during the Term.

4.7. Royalty payments shall be made to the applicable designated bank account of Licensor in the currency as specified below, or as may be otherwise notified by Licensor to Licensee:

4.8. Licensee on behalf of itself and its Affiliates, shall submit a written report signed by a person duly authorized by Licensee to Licensor within forty-five (45) days of the Date (with day 1 being the Date) using the template report as in **Annex A** for each type of Licensed Product Sold from 1 January 2013 (the Effective Date) and through the most recent complete calendar quarter ending prior to the Date. Thereafter Licensee, on behalf of itself and its Affiliates, shall for the Term continue to submit such written reports (in the format as previously specified in Annex A) for each subsequent calendar quarter within forty-five (45) days of the end of any such calendar quarter, or on termination of this Agreement, within forty-five (45) days of such termination date. Licensee warrants that each such report shall be complete and accurate and shall be signed by a duly authorized person and provided to Licensor in accordance with the aforementioned timeframes.

4.9. All sums due under this Agreement shall be exclusive of any value added tax, or any other additional sales tax or duty which shall be payable on the rendering by Licensor of an appropriate invoice to Licensee. Any and all other taxes, levies, charges, duties or fees shall be paid by the Party required to do so by applicable law. Specifically, Licensor will be responsible for any taxes to which it is subject as a result of the receipt of royalties made by Licensee to Licensor under this Agreement.

4.10. For any currency conversion from the currency of one country in which the Licensed Products are sold into U.S. Dollars required in determining the royalties due hereunder, such conversion shall be calculated at the conversion rate as reported in the *Wall Street*

Journal (New York Edition) on the last business day of the applicable quarterly period in which the royalties are determined, or such other method agreed to by the Parties in writing.

4.11. Licensor acknowledges and agrees to provide its business registration certificate to Licensee as required by mandatory Chinese law or regulations prior to Licensee's first payment, and Licensee will work with Licensor to identify the correct business registration certificate.

4.12. For any payment made pursuant to this Agreement, including interest on any overdue payment(s), the Parties acknowledge that the Chinese authorities and Chinese banking laws require certain formalities to be met before a payment can be made. If required, Licensee shall have a translation prepared of this Agreement for Chinese authorities. If there are any other formalities required by the Chinese authorities or the bank in China, the Parties will work together to resolve the issue as quickly as possible so that payments can be made in a timely manner.

4.13. Any withholding taxes levied in China upon payment by Licensee to Licensor of any sums hereunder and required to be withheld from such payment shall be withheld and paid by Licensee to the appropriate Chinese tax authorities. Within sixty (60) days after such payment, Licensee shall inform Licensor of the date and amount of the deduction made and shall forward to Licensor all receipts issued by the Chinese tax authorities, including the official receipts, save always that if any such receipts are issued by the Chinese tax authorities more than sixty (60) days after payment thereof, then Licensee shall forward them to Licensor within fourteen (14) days of receipt. In connection therewith, the gross amounts to be paid under this Agreement shall be adjusted for such Chinese withholding taxes to be borne by Licensor and its Affiliates. Should Licensor elect to pursue a claim for tax credit with the Chinese authorities, Licensee shall reasonably cooperate with and support Licensor, including doing all such further actions and acts as may be reasonably necessary in connection therewith. Any and all other taxes, levies, charges, duties or fees shall be paid by the Party required to do so by applicable law.

5. Record and Audit

5.1. Licensee shall, and shall procure that its Affiliates shall, keep accurate and complete books and records which relate to the Licensed Products in sufficient detail (consistent with generally accepted accounting practices for the industry) to enable the royalties payable hereunder to be determined. Such books and records, shall include, at a minimum, all records and accounts as may, under internationally recognised accounting practices, contain information bearing upon the amount of royalties payable in accordance with this Agreement, and be kept by Licensee for a period of three (3) years after the calendar quarter to which the books and records apply (but not more than 2 years after any termination of this Agreement).

5.2. Licensor shall have the right at any time during the Term and for 2 years thereafter, upon the provision of at least thirty (30) days' notice from Licensor, to nominate, at its own expense, a Third Party independent auditor, acceptable to Licensee (such acceptance not to be unreasonably withheld and where the said auditor is either PWC, DLT, KMPG and EY shall be deemed automatically given with the exception that Huawei may remove one auditor from this list based upon conflict of interest concerns) to examine and audit any and all books and records to the extent relevant to determination of the royalties paid in any specified period at the premises of Licensee. The audit shall be conducted during Licensee's normal business hours and without undue interference with Licensee's normal business. Any such audit shall take place no more than once per calendar year, and any particular calendar quarter shall be audited only once.

5.3. The auditor shall conduct the audit on consecutive days and shall complete the audit within a reasonable period, and Licensee shall assemble in a single location all books and records necessary for such audit to be carried out and make such personnel available as may be reasonably necessary to answer the questions of the auditor.

5.4. The Third Party auditor shall sign a non-disclosure agreement on reasonable terms to be discussed and agreed between said Third Party auditor and Licensee in advance of the commencement of any audit. Licensee shall have the right to refuse further access to confidential information in case it is demonstrable that the auditor is in breach of its confidentiality obligation.

5.5. Any independent auditor is authorised to report to Licensor, only whether Licensee is or is not (and if not, in what manner and the amount of underpayment) in compliance with its obligations in this Agreement and shall not disclose to Licensor or any Third Party any other information obtained during the audit. When providing the final audit report to Licensor, the auditor shall also furnish Licensee with a copy of such report.

5.6. Licensor shall use the information resulting from such audits exclusively for the implementation of, and ensuring compliance with, this Agreement and shall treat such information confidentially with the same degree of care as is used with respect to Licensor's own equally important confidential information to avoid disclosure to any Third Party.

5.7. If an overpayment is identified during such audit, Licensor will credit the amount overpaid to Licensee against the next payment due under this Agreement. To the extent that no further payment is due under this Agreement, Licensor shall within sixty (60) days after the later of (i) such determination or (ii) receipt of an invoice from Licensee, pay Licensee the amount by which royalties were determined to be overpaid. In the event that the audit identifies any underpayment, then the Parties shall meet and confer within thirty (30) days of such audit determination to discuss such underpayment, during which Licensee will provide such data and evidence it considers reasonably necessary to support its position, subject to Licensor agreeing to keep any such material confidential. Without prejudice to any other remedies available to the Parties (including dispute resolution in accordance with Section 10 of this Agreement), after such thirty (30) days, Licensee shall within thirty (30) days after the later of (i) such determination or (ii) receipt of an invoice from Licensor, pay Licensor the shortfall plus the interest specified at Section 5.8 on the amounts which such royalties were underpaid. In the event that any underpayment for the audit period exceeds five percent (5%) of the royalty amount actually due, Licensee shall bear the actual cost of the audit and Licensor shall share with Licensee copies of invoices of the auditor as evidence thereof.

5.8. Licensee shall be liable for interest on any overdue payment required to be made pursuant to this Section 5. Such interest shall commence on the date such payment becomes due until such payment is made, at an annual rate of five percent (5%). If at any time such interest rate exceeds the maximum legal rate in the jurisdiction where a claim therefore is being asserted, the interest rate shall be reduced to such maximum legal rate.

5.9. Licensor's rights of audit as set out in this Section 5 shall survive for two (2) years after the termination of the Agreement provided, however, that there shall be no right to audit for a time period for which an audit has been completed.

6. Term and Termination

6.1. This Agreement shall come into force upon the Date and shall remain in effect during the Term.

6.2. A Party may terminate this Agreement by written notice if the other Party (or an Affiliate) at any time commits a material breach of any of its significant obligations under this Agreement (which shall expressly include any non-payment) and, in the event of a breach capable of remedy, fails to cure, or procure the cure of, such breach within thirty (30) days after receipt of a notice specifying the nature of such breach and requiring remedy of the same.

6.3. A Party shall provide written notice to the other Party immediately upon the occurrence of any of the following events: (i) its insolvency, bankruptcy or liquidation or filing of any application therefor, or other commitment of an affirmative act of insolvency; (ii) attachment, execution or seizure of substantially all of the assets of the notifying Party or filing of any application therefor; (iii) assignment or transfer of that portion of the business to which this Agreement pertains to a trustee for the benefit of creditors; (iv) termination of its business or dissolution; or (v) in the case of Licensee, within ninety (90) days after the closing of a merger, acquisition, consolidation, transfer or otherwise wherein more than fifty percent (50%) of the ownership or Control of Licensee is acquired by an Entity then engaged in the manufacture or sale of End User Devices. The other Party shall have the right to terminate this Agreement with immediate effect by giving written notice of termination at any time upon such occurrence.

6.4. All licenses and rights granted hereunder shall be terminated, provided always that any rights and releases which occur before termination shall remain unaffected SAVE ALWAYS that the foregoing shall not be deemed to limit either Party's right to specifically enforce this Agreement, or to recover damages resulting from any breach of this Agreement by the other Party. The Parties agree that the failure to identify in this Agreement the breach of any particular obligation as a "material breach" does not preclude any Party from contending in the future that such breach is "material."

7. Assignment

7.1. From the Date:-

7.1.1. nothing contained herein shall prohibit Licensor from selling or assigning any Licensed Patent, provided that Licensor shall procure from its buyer or assignee that any such sale or assignment of any such Licensed Patent shall still be subject to the license, covenant and release granted to Licensee herein;

7.1.2. if Licensor or any of its Affiliates transfers its business in whole or in part through divestiture, merger or otherwise to a Third Party, Licensor shall procure, prior to the divestiture, that the license, covenant and release granted to Licensee under this Agreement shall continue (as if no such divestiture occurs) for the Term; and

7.1.3. if any of Licensor's Affiliates ceases to be its Affiliate and owns or controls any Licensed Patents, Licensor shall procure, prior to the Affiliate ceasing to be an Affiliate that such licenses, covenant and release (if any) continue for the Term.

7.2. Notwithstanding Sections 7.1.1-7.1.3 above, in the event that any successor-in-interests or assigns of Licensor ("Assignees") make any claim or assertion in a legal proceeding or otherwise against Licensee or its Affiliates or any of their past or present customers, distributors, retailers or end users, Licensor shall immediately investigate the facts and provide information to Licensee upon the request of Licensee, shall use its commercially reasonable best efforts to ensure compliance with Sections 7.1.1-7.1.3 by Assignees and shall indemnify Licensee from any such claims and assertions, including directly intervening in any such claim or legal proceedings. In addition, Licensee shall allow this Agreement to be introduced in evidence in any litigation (with confidentiality safeguards) brought by an Assignee of Licensed Patents, in any case where this Agreement would be a defence to infringement of such assigned Licensed Patents.

7.3. Save as otherwise set out herein neither Party may grant or assign any rights or delegate any obligations under this Agreement to any Third Party (save to an Affiliate) without the prior written consent of the other, which shall not be unreasonably withheld, and any attempted assignment without such consent shall be null and void. In the event Licensor consents to Licensee assigning any rights or delegating any obligations under this Agreement to a Third Party acquiring the Licensee business in whole or in part through divestiture, merger or otherwise, its shall be expressly understood that the rights assigned and/or obligations delegated shall not extend beyond those possessed by Licensee at the time of the acquisition and shall expressly exclude the acquiring Third Party's business at the time of acquisition.

8. Representations

8.1. Licensor hereby represents and warrants that (i) it has received all necessary corporate approvals and that the signatory below is duly authorized to execute this Agreement on behalf of Licensor; (ii) Licensor and/or its Affiliates own and have the right to license the Licensed Patents licensed to Licensee hereunder; and (iii) it has not made and shall not make any agreements, assignments or encumbrances inconsistent with the provisions of this Agreement.

8.2. Licensee hereby represents and warrants that (i) it has received all necessary corporate approvals and that the signatory below is duly authorized to execute this Agreement on behalf of Licensee; and (ii) it has not made and shall not make any outstanding agreements, assignments or encumbrances inconsistent with the provisions of this Agreement.

8.3. Nothing contained in this Agreement shall be construed as:

8.3.1. a warranty or representation either expressed or implied by either Party as to the validity, enforceability or scope of any Licensed Patent herein;

8.3.2. an agreement to bring or prosecute actions or suits against third parties for infringement; or

8.3.3. conferring any right to use, in advertising, publicity or otherwise, any name, trade name, trademark, or any contraction, abbreviation or simulation thereof.

and except as expressly set forth herein, neither Party makes any representations nor extends any warranties of any kind, either express or implied.

9. Applicable Law and Dispute Resolution

9.1. This Agreement shall be governed by and construed in accordance with the substantive law of England & Wales without regard to conflicts of law rules.

9.2. In the event of any and all disputes arising under, out of or in connection with this Agreement (including any Annex and any amendment made thereto), including any question regarding its existence, validity or termination, representatives of both Parties shall enter into good faith negotiations with the aim of resolving the dispute. An attempt to arrive at a settlement shall be deemed to have failed as soon as one Party so notifies the other Party in writing. Such notification shall not be sent earlier than thirty (30) days after the dispute arises. Provided always that nothing in the foregoing will prevent a Party from commencing proceedings for the purpose of seeking interim or pre-emptive relief on an emergency basis.

9.3. The High Court of England and Wales shall have non-exclusive jurisdiction to finally settle all disputes, differences or questions arising out of or relating to the interpretation or performance of this Agreement between the Parties.

10. Notices

Any and all notices, requests, demands, consents, agreements and other communications required or permitted to be given or made under this Agreement shall be given in writing and in the English language and shall be (i) delivered personally; or (ii) sent by facsimile; or (iii) mailed by registered mail; or (v) delivered by courier to the following addresses of the Parties or to such other address as the Party concerned may subsequently notify in writing to the other Party in accordance with this Section 11.

Unless otherwise specifically provided for in this Agreement, such communications shall take effect upon receipt by the addressee, provided such communications shall be deemed to have been duly given or made and shall be deemed to have been received by a Party: (i) if delivered personally, at delivery; (ii) if mailed by registered mail, unless actually received earlier, on the expiration of seven (7) days after the date of mailing; (iii) on the day of the receipt of sender's facsimile confirmation of the transmission in case of facsimile; or (iv) if delivered by courier, on the date of delivery.

11. Non-waiver

Neither this Agreement nor any provision hereof may be waived without the prior written consent of the Party against whom such waiver is asserted. No delay or omission by either Party to exercise or assert any right or power shall impair any such right or power to be construed to be a waiver thereof. Consent by either Party to, or waiver of, a breach by the other Party shall not constitute consent to, waiver of, or excuse for any other different or subsequent breach.

12. Force Majeure

Neither Party shall be in default or liable for any loss or damage resulting from delays in performance or from failure to perform or comply with terms of this Agreement due to any unforeseeable, unavoidable and unpreventable causes, which causes include but are not limited to Acts of God; riots and insurrections; natural catastrophe; social unrest; war; fire; strikes and other labour difficulties (whether or not the Party is in a position to concede to such demands); embargoes; judicial action; lack of or inability to obtain export permits or approvals; and acts of civil or military authorities.

13. Miscellaneous

13.1. This Agreement, and its Annexes, constitutes the entire and only agreement between the Parties with respect to the subject matter hereof and merges and supersedes all prior and contemporaneous oral or written discussions, negotiations, understandings, representations, warranties and agreements of the Parties.

13.2. Any amendment or modification of any of the provisions of this Agreement or any right, power or remedy hereunder shall not be effective unless made in writing and signed by authorized representatives of both Parties.

13.3. This Agreement is considered to be jointly drafted and neither Party shall benefit from who actually drafted the Agreement.

13.4. Notwithstanding any termination or expiration of this Agreement, any Section set forth in this Agreement remaining to be performed in whole or in part, capable of taking effect following termination, or which by its nature is contemplated to survive the termination or expiration of this Agreement shall survive and continue in full force and effect despite termination or expiration.

13.5. If any of the provisions of this Agreement is or becomes invalid, illegal or unenforceable, the validity, legality, and enforceability of any other provision of this Agreement shall in no way be affected or impaired thereby, and such invalid or unenforceable term, Section or provision shall be deemed deleted from this Agreement, and this Agreement shall continue in full force and effect. Should such case arise, the Parties shall negotiate in good faith a replacement but legally valid, term, Section or provision that best meets the intent of the Parties.

13.6. Save as otherwise set out herein, nothing in this Agreement precludes Licensee from challenging or denying the validity of any Licensed Patent by filing or participating in an opposition, an invalidity action or any declaratory judgment action challenging or denying the validity of such claim.

13.7. The relationship between Licensor and Licensee is that of independent contractors. Licensor and Licensee are not joint ventures, partners, principal and agent, master and servant, employer or employee, and have no other relationship other than independent contracting parties. Each Party is executing this Agreement solely on behalf of itself and its Affiliates and is not acting on behalf of, and does not represent, any other company or entity or any government agency. Nothing in this Agreement shall be construed as creating a partnership, joint venture, or other formal business organization of any kind.

13.8. Each Party agrees, upon reasonable request by the other Party, to consent to the registration of this Agreement to the extent required by the laws of the applicable jurisdiction requiring registration and subject always to the terms herein.

13.9. This Agreement may be executed in counterparts in the English language and each such counterpart shall be deemed an original thereof. Facsimile signatures or signatures delivered by e-mail in.pdf or similar format will be deemed original signatures for purposes of this Agreement.

13.10. The headings and sub-headings of the Sections are inserted for convenience or reference only and are not intended to be a part of or to affect the meaning or interpretation of this Agreement.

IN WITNESS WHEREOF, the Parties hereto have caused this Agreement to be signed by their duly authorized representatives and executed on the Date.

Huawei Technologies Co., Ltd.	**Unwired Planet Limited Liability Company**
Name	Name
Title	Title
Signature	Signature

Annex A—Reporting Template

Huawei Technologies Co., Ltd. and Huawei Technologies (UK) Co., Ltd ("Licensee") is providing the below information pursuant to the terms of the patent license agreement between Unwired Planet Limited Liability Company, Unwired Planet International Limited, Huawei Technologies Co., Ltd. and Huawei Technologies (UK) Co., Ltd. ("Agreement"). This report relates to the period [[INSERT]—[INSERT]][calendar year ending [INSERT]]

For [Insert applicable reporting entity] in _________:

Specify End User Terminal	**Standards Complied to (2G, 3G, 4G etc.)**	**Total units Sold**	**Total selling price (with no deductions) in currency sold at**	**Selling Price (with permitted deductions specified in this Agreement) in currency sold at**		**Royalties (including all exchange rate conversion calculations)**
Total in applicable currency						

Appendix B2

Patent License Agreement Terms
TCL Communication Technology Holdings, Ltd v. Telefonaktiebolaget LM Ericsson, Case No. 8:14-CV-00341 JVS-DFMx (C.D. Cal. Dec. 22, 2017)
From Amended Final Judgment and Injunction
AGREEMENT

DEFINITIONS

For the purpose of this [Agreement], the following definitions shall apply: "Affiliate" of a Party means a company or other legal entity which is controlled by the Party. For the purpose of this definition, "control" shall mean direct or indirect ownership of more than fifty percent (50%) of the voting power, capital, or other securities of the controlled or commonly controlled entity. "Brand Company" means a company or other legal entity, other than a Network Operator, which is active in the consumer electronics business and/or wireless communications business and/or IT industry.

"Components" means any item of equipment, including, for example, a sub- system, sub-assembly or component, in software, hardware, and/or firmware form, of any TCL Product, which is sold, licensed, or supplied, or intended to be sold, licensed, or supplied, to a Third Party other than as a complete and ready to use end-use item, for example, because it requires additional industrial, manufacturing, or assembly processes before being used or sold as an end-use item, and is intended for incorporation into any product. Examples of Components include, but are by no means limited to, platforms, ASICs and chipsets, modules, printed circuit boards, integrated circuits, semiconductor devices, processors, multi-core processors, multi-chip modules, and multi-chip packages, embedded modules and core engines. This definition of "Components" shall exclude any product employed for the purpose of repair or upgrade of already sold products which are licensed under this Agreement. "Consumer" means a natural person who buys products as a final user.

"Costs of Insurance and Transportation" means TCL's, as the case may be, actual direct costs of insurance and transportation to ship TCL Products to its customers. For the avoidance of doubt, Costs of Insurance and Transportation shall not include any labor fee or any overhead costs of any kind.

"Effective Date" means the date of [this Agreement].

"End User Terminal" means a complete and ready to use device or Knocked Down version of such complete device with the largest of the width, length, and depth of such complete device in its most compact form being 250 mm or less, which can be directly used by a Consumer for wireless communications (i.e. to receive and transmit information over the air by means of using one or more of the Standards), without the device having to be integrated or embedded into another device or connected to another device through, for example, a USB, PCMCIA, memory card, WLAN, or Bluetooth interface. For the avoidance of all doubt, the term "End User Terminal" does not mean subassemblies or parts of products such as, but not limited to, Components, other than as sold as part of the End User Terminal or as spare parts or repair parts of already Sold End User Terminals. For the further avoidance of doubt, TCL is not required to pay any royalty to Ericsson for such spare parts or repair parts of already Sold End User Terminals.

"Entity" means any individual, firm, company, corporation, or other corporate or legal entity (wherever and however incorporated or established), government, state, agency or agency of a state, local or municipal authority or government body or any joint venture, association or partnership (whether or not having a separate legal personality).

"Ericsson" means Defendants and Counterclaim Plaintiffs Telefonaktiebolaget LM Ericsson, a company established under the laws of Sweden, with organization number 556016-0680, with its registered office at SE-164 83 Stockholm, Sweden; Ericsson Inc., a Delaware corporation headquartered at 6300 Legacy Drive, Plano, Texas 75024; and all of their Affiliates.

"External Modem" means a separate external Consumer device which can be connected to or inserted into an external slot of another device by an individual consumer (i.e. not an entity of any kind) through, for example, a USB, PCMCIA, memory card, WiFi, or Bluetooth interface, in order to allow said another device to communicate by means of any or more of the Standards. The External Modem may not be designed for the purpose of being embedded into such other device or may not in itself include an immediate physical user- interface to an individual Consumer to transmit or receive wireless data and/or voice transmissions by means of any or more of the Standards (such a device shall fall under the definition of End User Terminal). The term "External Modem" does not include Components (other than as sold incorporated into the External Modem or sold as part of a kit of External Modem) or modules.

"Future Standards" means the agreed protocols by ETSI, ARIS, T1P1, CCSA, and/or other relevant telecommunications standards setting bodies that are applicable to UMB, WiMax IEEE802.16m, and/or any other beyond 4G standards, irrespective of the transmission medium or frequency band, as well as any updates in respect of such protocols.

"Have Made" means the right to have a Third Party make a product for the use and benefit of the party exercising the have made right provided all of the following conditions are fulfilled: (a) the party exercising the have made right owns and supplies the designs, specifications and working drawings supplied to such Third Party; and (b) such designs, specifications and working drawings are, complete and sufficient so that no substantial additional design, specification and working drawings are needed by any Third Party; and (c) such Third Party is not allowed to sell such product to other third parties.

"Knocked Down" means a complete End User Terminal product in the form of complete knocked down or semi-knocked down kits of parts, including complete and substantially complete kits of parts, where such kit of part or knocked down product is always a complete and ready to use End User Terminal.

"License Period" means the period commencing on the Effective Date and having a period of five (5) years calculated from the Effective Date.

"Licensed Patents" means those Patents (in any country of the world) as to which it is, or is claimed by the owner to be, not possible, on technical grounds taking into account normal technical practice and the state of the art generally available at the time of adoption or publication of the relevant Standards, to make, sell, lease, or otherwise dispose of, repair, use, or operate equipment or methods which comply with the relevant Standards, without infringing such Patents.

"Network Operator" means an Entity, including such Entity's Affiliates, that as its main business (a) owns or licenses frequency spectrum, directly or indirectly, from a government or other relevant authority or Entity, and offers wireless data- or telecommunications services to Consumers over such owned or licensed spectrum; and/or (b) offers wired data- or telecommunications services to Consumers.

"Net Selling Price" means the greater of (a) the selling price actually obtained for the TCL Product in the form in which it is Sold, and (b) the selling price which a seller would realize from an un-Affiliated buyer in an arm's length sale of an equivalent product in the same quantity and at the same time and place as such Sale, whether or not assembled and without excluding therefrom any components or subassemblies thereof. In determining the "Net Selling Price," only the following shall be excluded to the extent actually included in the selling price obtained for such products: (i) Usual Trade Discounts actually allowed to non-Affiliated persons or entities; (ii) Packing Costs; (iii) Costs of Insurance and Transportation; and (iv) Taxes and Custom Duties. For the avoidance of doubt, allowed deductions for Usual Trade Discounts, Packaging Costs, and Costs of Insurance and Transportation shall in total not exceed eight (8) percent units of the selling price.

"Packing Costs" means TCL's, as the case may be, actual direct costs of packing and/or packaging TCL Products for shipment to its customer. For the avoidance of doubt, Packing Costs shall include extra batteries, charger, ear phones, SO card, user manual (in any form including but not limited to CD- ROM), warranty card, USB cable, welcome kit, packing box, labels, protective screen cover, plastic bags, carrying kit and separate additional phone cover case. For the avoidance of doubt, Packing Costs shall not include any labor fee or any overhead costs of any kind.

"Party/Parties" means Ericsson and TCL.

"Patents" means patent claims (including claims of licensable patent applications), and like statutory rights other than design patents, owned, or controlled by Ericsson at any time during the License Period.

"Personal Computer" means a complete and ready to use device, designed mainly for data processing by means of a physical or virtual keyboard, with the largest of the width, length, and depth of such complete device in its most compact form being more than 250 mm, which can be directly used by a Consumer for wireless communications (i.e. to receive and transmit information over the air by means of using any or more of the Standards), without the device having to be integrated or embedded into another device or connected to another device through for example a USB, memory card, WLAN, or Bluetooth interface. For the avoidance of all doubts, the term "Personal Computer" does not mean subassemblies or parts or products such as, but not limited to Intermediate Products, other than as sold as part of the Personal Computer or as spare parts or repair parts of already Sold Personal Computers.

"Retailer" means an Entity, including such Entity's Affiliates, other than a Brand Company, a licensee of Ericsson, or a Network Operator, which is having as its main business to sell Third Party branded products to Consumers whether through shops or online.

"Sale," "Sell," "Sold," or any similar term, mean the delivery of TCL Products in any country of the world to a Third Party regardless of the basis for compensation, if any, including lease, rent or similar transaction, whether as an individual item or as a component or constituent of other products, or the putting into use of the TCL Products by TCL for any purpose other than routine testing thereof—with a Sale being deemed to have occurred upon shipment or invoicing or such putting into use, whichever shall first occur. TCL Products that are returned for refund (for avoidance of doubt to exclude warranty returns), may be netted against units Sold, so long as a returned unit that is subsequently resold is counted as a new Sale.

"Standards" means the ETSI (or, if applicable, its equivalent internationally recognized body or organization) cellular telecommunication standards 2G, 3G and 4G. For the avoidance of any doubt, Standards does not include WiFi, WiMax, CDMA, or Future Standards.

"Taxes and Custom Duties" means import, export, excise, sales and value added taxes and custom duties levied or imposed directly upon the Sale of TCL Products that TCL, as the case may be, remits to the government body levying or imposing such taxes or duties.

"TCL" means Plaintiffs and Counterclaim Defendants TCL Communication Technology Holdings Ltd., a company established under the laws of Cayman Islands, with its registered office at Cricket Square, Hutchins Drive, P.O. Box 2681, Grand Cayman KY1-1111, Cayman Islands; TCT Mobile (US) Inc., a Delaware corporation headquartered at 25 Edelman, Irvine, CA 92618; TCT Mobile Limited, a company established under the laws of Hong Kong, having its registered office at Room 1502, Tower 6, China Hong Kong City, 33 Canton Road, Tsimshatsui, Kowloon, Hong Kong; and all of their Affiliates.

"TCL Products" shall mean the End-User Terminals, External Modems, and Personal Computers all being branded with (a) a brand owned by TCL, Network Operators, or Retailers, provided that such TCL Products are not also branded with a brand owned by a Brand Company; (b) a brand licensed to TCL, Network Operators, or Retailer, provided that such licensed brand is not owned by a Brand Company; or (c) TCL shall have the option to ask for permission from Ericsson to add End User Terminals branded with Third Party brands (not being a Brand Company or a licensee of Ericsson) to the definition of TCL Products on a case by case basis. Such addition of End User Terminals branded with a Third Party brand (not being a Brand Company or a licensee of Ericsson) is always subject to Ericsson prior written approval. Such approval is at Ericsson's sole discretion. Notwithstanding the above, TCL Products branded with a brand licensed or transferred to it from Alcatel, Alcatel Lucent, or Blackberry Sold after such license or transfer and are compliant with one or more of the Standards shall be included in this definition of TCL Products and subject to royalty payment in accordance with this Agreement.

"Third Party/Third Parties" shall mean any Entity that is not Ericsson or TCL. "Usual Trade Discounts" shall mean discounts actually allowed by TCL, as the case may be, to un-Affiliated persons or entities for TCL Products Sold by TCL, as the case may be, to such person or entity solely to the extent such discounts are agreed upon in writing by TCL, as the case may be, and such person or entity in a written supply (or related) agreement on, or prior to the time of Sale of such TCL Product, including prompt-pay discounts, volume discounts, price protection discounts, stock balancing discounts, late delivery penalties, payments for promotional rebates provided by such person or entity to its end user customers (the "Trade Discount Deductions"). Notwithstanding anything to the contrary above, the following shall not be included in the Trade Discount Deductions: discounts/payments agreed upon after the time of Sale of a TCL Product and market development and/or business development funds. "2G" shall mean Global System for Mobile Communications (GSM) and Generalized Packet Radio System (GPRS), including the Enhanced GPRS (E- GPRS/ EDGE) standard specifications released or published by 3GPP and/or relevant local standardization bodies such as ETSI, TIA, T1P1, ARIB, TIC, and CCSA, irrespective of the transmission medium or frequency band, at the time of the Effective Date and thereafter as well as updates in respect of such standard specifications during the License Period. For the avoidance of any doubt, 2G does not include 3G or any Future Standards.

"3G" shall mean UTRA FDD mode, i.e. UMTS and WCDMA, including HSPA standard specifications released or published by 3GPP and/or relevant local standardization bodies such as ETSI, TIA, T1P1, ARIS, TTC, and CCSA, irrespective of the transmission medium or frequency band, at the time of the Effective Date and thereafter, as well as any updates in respect of such standard specifications during the License Period. For the avoidance of any doubt, 3G does not include 2G, CDMA, WiMax, WiFi, or any Future Standards.

"4G" shall mean E-UTRA (FOO mode and TDD mode (including but not limited to LTE or TD-LTE)) standard specifications released or published by 3GPP and/or relevant local standardization bodies such as but not limited to ETSI, TIA, T1P1, ARIB, TTC, and CCSA, irrespective of the transmission medium or frequency band, at the time of the Effective Date and thereafter, as well as any updates in respect of such standard specifications during the License Period. However, such updates may not extend to any Future Standards. For the avoidance of any doubt, 4G does not include 2G, 3G, CDMA, WiMax, WiFi, or Future Standards.

"WiFi" shall mean the 802.11 standard specifications released or published by IEEE irrespective of the transmission medium, frequency band, or duplexing scheme, at the lime of the Effective Date, as well as any updates in respect of such standard specifications during the License Period. However, such updates may not extend to any Future Standards. For the avoidance of any doubt, WiFi does not include 2G, 3G, 4G, CDMA, WiMax, or Future Standards.

"WiMax" shall mean the 802.16 standard specifications released or published by IEEE, irrespective of the transmission medium, frequency band or duplexing scheme, at the time of the Effective Date, as well as any updates in respect of such standard specifications during the License Period. However, such updates may not extend to any Future Standards. For the avoidance of any doubt, WiMax does not include 2G, 3G, 4G, CDMA, WiFi, or Future Standards.

"CDMA" shall mean CDMA2000 standard specifications released or published by 3GPP2 and/or relevant local standardization bodies such as but not limited to ETSI, TIA, T1P1, ARIB, TTC, and CCSA, irrespective of the transmission medium, frequency band or duplexing scheme, at the time of the Effective Date, as well as any updates in respect of such standard specifications during the License Period. However, such updates may not extend to any Future Standards. For the avoidance of any doubt, CDMA does not include 2G, 3G, 4G, WiMax, WiFi, or Future Standards.

TERMS

A. License Grant

License Grant. Subject to the terms and conditions of this Agreement, TCL hereby is granted a world-wide, non-transferable, and non-exclusive license under Ericsson's Licensed Patents to make, Have Made, use, import, Sell, and offer for Sale TCL Products. The license and rights granted to TCL granted by this Agreement shall expire at the end of the License Period. The license granted to TCL further includes the right to make, use, and import solely by TCL (but not to Sell, lease, or otherwise dispose of to Third Parties) manufacturing and testing equipment compliant with the Standards for the testing, developing, and manufacturing of TCL Products.

Sublicense. TCL shall grant sublicenses of the rights set forth in this Clause to all future Affiliates of TCL Selling TCL Products. TCL shall procure that such future Affiliate shall be bound in all respects to all of the obligations contained in this Agreement, including but not limited to, the payment of royalties as set forth in Clause E of this Agreement. TCL shall be liable for the payment of royalties as set forth in Clause E attributed to all sublicensed future Affiliates, which shall be effectuated by TCL Communication Technology Holdings Ltd. directly. Any sublicense granted hereunder shall terminate if the Affiliate ceases to be an Affiliate of TCL.

No Implied License. Nothing in this Agreement shall be construed as a right to use or sell TCL Products in a manner which conveys or purports to convey whether explicitly, by principles of implied license, or otherwise, any rights to any Third Party user or purchaser of the TCL Products, under any patent of Ericsson covering or relating to any combination of the TCL Products with any other product (not licensed hereunder) where the right applies specifically to the combination and not to the TCL Product itself.

No Rights to Provide Foundry Services. For the avoidance of all doubt, nothing in this Agreement shall mean that Ericsson is granting a license under any Licensed Patents to TCL for providing of foundry services to Third Parties, i.e. TCL manufacturing and selling products based upon Third Party made and owned design when the product is thereafter sold to or directly on behalf of such same Third Party.

B. Limitations of License Grant

Jointly Owned Patents. With respect to Patents licensed herein which are owned jointly by Ericsson with others, the Court recognizes that there are countries which require the express consent of all inventors or their assignees to the grant of licenses or rights under patents issued in such countries for such jointly owned inventions. Ericsson shall give such consent and shall use all reasonable efforts to obtain such consent from its employees, and from other Third Parties and future Affiliates, as required to make full and effective any such licenses and rights granted.

If, in spite of such efforts, Ericsson is unable to obtain such consents from any such employees or Third Parties, the resulting inability of Ericsson to make full and effective its purported grant of such licenses and rights shall not be considered to be a breach of this Agreement. For the avoidance of doubt, in such a case, the licenses and rights shall be considered granted by Ericsson to the maximum extent possible, and, consequently, if TCL acquires a corresponding license from the employee or Third Party, TCL shall be deemed licensed under the patent.

No Rights Against Infringers. There may be countries in which TCL may have, as a consequence of this Agreement, rights against infringers of Ericsson's Patents licensed hereunder. TCL shall not assert any such right it may have by reason of any Third Party's infringement of any such Patents.

C. Release

Upon the receipt by Ericsson of the release payments set forth in Clause E by TCL, Ericsson shall release TCL and all customers of TCL who have purchased or used products herein licensed to TCL from claims for past patent infringement, provided such act would be licensed under this Agreement if it had occurred subsequent to the Effective Date.

Within thirty (30) days of final judgment (inclusive of all appeals and post-trial proceedings) and provided that Ericsson has received the release payment set forth in this Agreement from TCL, the parties shall cooperate to promptly seek the dismissal (with prejudice where available) of all claims and counterclaims in all litigations covered by the Court's anti-suit injunction dated July 10, 2015.

D. Know-How and Trade Secrets

No license or other right is granted herein to TCL, directly or by implication, estoppels or otherwise, with respect to any trade secrets or know-how, and no such license or other right shall arise from the consummation of this Agreement or from any acts, statements or dealings leading to such consummation. Except as specifically provided herein, Ericsson is not required by this Agreement to furnish or disclose to TCL any technical or other information.

E. Payments, Report, and Audit

Royalties. In consideration of the license granted herein, TCL shall pay Ericsson:

1. A release payment of $16,449, 071 for past unlicensed sales of End User Terminals compliant with 2G, 3G, and/or 4G for the period 2007 through 2015, to be paid within thirty (30) days of the Effective Date;

2. A release payment for past unlicensed sales of End User Terminals compliant with 2G, 3G, and/or 4G for the period 2016 through 2017, to be reported and paid in January and February 2018, as set forth in the "Reports" and "Payment" section herein; and
3. A running royalty for End User Terminals Sold beginning January 1, 2018 according to the following schedule:
   a. For each such product Sold that is compliant with GSM, GPRS, or EDGE (but not compliant with WCDMA, HSPA, and/or 4G), 0.164% of the Net Selling Price if sold in the United States, 0.118% of the Net Selling Price if sold in Europe, and 0.090% of the Net Selling Price if sold anywhere in the world other than the United States or Europe;
   b. For each such product Sold that is compliant with WCDMA or HSPA (but not compliant with 4G), 0.300% of the Net Selling Price if sold in the United States, 0.264% of the Net Selling Price if sold in Europe, and 0.224% of the Net Selling Price if sold anywhere in the world other than the United States or Europe;
   c. For each such product Sold that is compliant with 4G, 0.450% of the Net Selling Price if sold in the United States, and 0.314% of the Net Selling Price if sold anywhere in the world other than the United States.

   Should TCL purchase TCL End User Terminals from a Third Party claiming to be licensed or to have pass-through rights under Ericsson Licensed Patents that confer a license covering the End User Terminal, then TCL will receive credit for that pass through license in the royalty rates applied. In particular, with regard to Ericsson Patents that are essential to the WCDMA Standards ("Ericsson WCDMA Licensed Patents") for the Selling of ASICs, then TCL may have the option of remaining unlicensed by Ericsson under such Ericsson WCDMA Licensed Patents subject to Selling TCL End User Terminals with ASICs that are compliant with the WCDMA Standard. TCL shall then pay a royalty equal to the rate paid for the GSM/GPRS/EDGE and/or LTE Standards as specified in Clause E(3)(a) or Clause E(3)(c) of this Agreement, as applicable, for each such TCL End User Terminal provided that such TCL End User Terminal is also compliant with any of the GSM/GPRS/EDGE Standards and/or LTE Standards while it is qualified as a WCDMA End User Terminal. For the avoidance of doubt, the Parties acknowledge the doctrine of patent exhaustion. Ericsson confirms that upon the Effective Date it has not provided any licenses with pass-through rights under its 4G patent portfolio to a chipset provider, making, using, importing, selling, or otherwise disposing of 4G compliant chipsets and components.

For the avoidance of doubt, TCL shall only be required to pay the highest prevailing royalty rate under this Agreement for each End User Terminal. For example, the 3G royalty rate for 3G multimode End User Terminal includes the royalty rate also for the 2G part in such End User Terminal.

This Agreement does not require TCL to pay any royalties for the Sale of any External Modems or Personal Computers that are compliant with 2G, 3G, and/or 4G during the release period (i.e., prior to January 1, 2018) or the License Period. TCL shall have a royalty-free license for all such sales.

Reports. TCL Communication Technology Holdings Ltd. shall, on behalf of all TCL Parties, make written reports to Ericsson for each applicable six months (January to June and July to December (each a "Reported Period")). Such reports shall be provided to Ericsson no later than one (1) calendar month after the first day of each January, and July for each year during the License Period and as of such dates including the last report after the License Period, stating in each such report, the number, Net Selling Price, gross price and other relevant information for each type of TCL Product Sold or otherwise disposed of during the preceding Reported Period, and on which royalty is payable as provided in this Clause E, and shall be at least as detailed as specified in Appendix 1. In addition to the written report, TCL Communication Technology Holdings Ltd. shall, on behalf of all TCL

Parties and TCL Affiliates, send such report in Excel-format (.xls format) to Ericsson via email to: ipr.unit@ericsson.com. In the event that no royalty payment is due for a Reported Period, TCL shall so report.

Payment. TCL Communication Technology Holdings Ltd. shall, on behalf of all TCL Parties and Affiliates, pay to Ericsson the royalties specified in this Agreement no later than two calendar months after the end of each Reported Period, i.e. no later than on February 28th and August 31st for TCL Products Sold during the preceding Reported Period. The payment to Ericsson shall be made to the Ericsson fully owned Affiliate Ericsson AB by wire transfer to the Ericsson bank account as specified in Appendix 2. Such payment to Ericsson AB shall fulfill TCL's payment obligations under the Agreement and Ericsson's claims for infringement of the '556 and '506 patents for the Reported Period that corresponds to the payment.

Ericsson shall have the right to assign any rights of Ericsson in relation to any receivables arising under this Agreement to any financial institution or other Third Party and may disclose confidential information related to this Agreement for such purpose. If required, the TCL shall provide acknowledgment over the assignment to the financial institution or other third party. For the avoidance of doubt, any such assignment shall in no way affect the obligations of TCL to Ericsson under this Agreement.

Records and Audits. TCL Communication Technology Holdings Ltd., on behalf of TCL and all Affiliates, shall keep records showing the sales or other disposition of products sold or otherwise disposed of in sufficient detail to enable the royalties payable by TCL to Ericsson to be determined, and further, on behalf of TCL and all Affiliates, shall permit its books and records to be examined to the extent necessary to verify that reports and payments are sufficiently made in accordance with the Agreement, such examination to be made by an independent and professional auditor agreed by the Parties, such appointment not to be unreasonably refused, withheld or delayed by TCL, and without a contingency fee arrangement between the to-be- appointed auditor and Ericsson based on the outcome of the audit amount to be collected. This shall at least include all books, records, and accounts as may under internationally recognized accounting practices contain information bearing upon the amount of royalties payable in accordance with this Agreement. If the auditor confirms, based on e.g. the books, records, information and accounts which are provided by TCL to the auditor in accordance with TCL's obligations in this Agreement, that TCL has underpaid, TCL shall pay such deficiency amount within thirty days after receipt of invoice from Ericsson. In the event there is an overpayment by TCL, Ericsson shall credit such overpayment, verified by the auditor, against future payments by TCL to Ericsson. For the avoidance of doubt, an audit shall be conducted no more than once every year and only upon ten (10) days prior written notice to TCL. The auditor shall use best efforts to conduct the audit in a manner that limits its interference with TCL's normal business activities and/or operations.

The cost of such audit shall be borne by Ericsson, unless such audit determines that TCL has underpaid the royalties due hereunder by the lesser of (a) more than five percent (5%) or (b) two hundred thousand U.S. Dollars ($200,000), in which case, TCL shall reimburse Ericsson for the reasonable cost of such audit. TCL shall preserve and maintain all such books and records required for audit for a period of five years after the calendar quarter for which the books and records apply.

The expiration of this Agreement shall not prejudice the right of Ericsson to conduct a final audit of the records of TCL, provided such audit is initiated no later than one (1) year from the expiration of the Agreement.

TCL Communication Technology Holdings Ltd., on behalf of TCL and all Affiliates, shall, at the agreed date for the auditor visit to the TCL premises, provide the auditor with the books and records, as requested by the auditor. The auditor shall have the right to analyze and verify such books and records at TCL's premises. For the avoidance of all doubt, such relevant books, records and accounts shall be treated as TCL confidential information

("TCL Audit Confidential Information") and any TCL Audit Confidential Information shall not be disclosed to Ericsson under any circumstances. Auditor shall use best efforts to observe the rules of on-site audit field work when in TCL premises.

Conversion to U.S. Dollars. To the extent that the Net Selling Price for TCL Products Sold is paid to TCL other than in U.S. Dollars then TCL shall convert the portion of the royalty payable to Ericsson from such Net Selling Price into U.S. Dollars at the official exchange rate of the currency of the country from which the Net Selling Price was paid, as quoted by the Financial Times for the last business day of the calendar quarter in which such TCL Products were Sold. If the transfer of or the conversion into U.S. Dollars is not lawful or possible, the payment of such part of the royalties as is necessary shall be made by the deposit thereof, in the currency of the country where the Sale was made on which the royalty was based to the credit and account of Ericsson or its nominee in any commercial bank or trust company of Ericsson's choice located in that country prompt notice of which shall be given by TCL to Ericsson.

Late Payments. TCL shall pay interest on any overdue payment required to be made pursuant to this Agreement, commencing on the date such payment becomes due, at an annual rate of twelve percent (12%).

Taxes. All payments required by this Agreement are exclusive of taxes, customs, or any other duties, and TCL shall be responsible for the payment of all such taxes, customs or other duties including, but not limited to, all sales, use, rental receipt, personal property or other taxes and their equivalents which may be levied or assessed in connection with this Agreement (excluding only taxes based on Ericsson's net income). Hence, if in accordance with present or future laws, Ericsson shall be obliged to pay, or TCL obliged to deduct from any payment to Ericsson, any amount with respect to any taxes, customs or any other duties levied, for which Ericsson is responsible as stated above, TCL shall increase the payment to Ericsson by an amount to cover such payment by Ericsson or deduction by TCL.

F. Change of Control

In the event that more than 20% of TCL's ownership changes by merger, acquisition, consolidation, transfer, or otherwise, any party may seek to address with the Court whether such change should impact the rights and obligations set forth in this Agreement, or whether modification, termination, or clarification of the Agreement is required regarding the parties' obligations given such change.

G. Transfer of Licensed Patents

Ericsson shall not transfer or assign any of the Licensed Patents during the License Period unless such assignment, including future assignments of any of the Licensed Patents, is made subject to maintenance of the licenses and rights as granted under this Agreement.

H. No Additional Limitations or Obligations

Nothing contained in this Agreement shall (i) limit the rights which TCL has outside the scope of the license and rights granted hereunder, or restrict the right of TCL to make, Have Made, use, lease, sell, or otherwise dispose of any particular product or products not licensed herein; (ii) obligate any Party to bring or prosecute actions or suits against Third Parties for infringement; (iii) obligate any Party to furnish any manufacturing or technical information or assistance; (iv) obligate any Party to file any patent application, or to secure any patent or patent rights, or to maintain any patent in force, or to provide copies of patent applications to the other Parties, or to disclose any inventions described or claimed in such patent applications; (v) confer any right to use, in advertising, publicity or otherwise, any name, trade name, trademark, or any contraction, abbreviation, or simulation thereof; (vi) obligate Ericsson to make any determination as to the applicability of any patent to any product of TCL; or (v) require Ericsson to assume any responsibilities whatsoever with respect to the manufacture, sale, lease, use, importation, or disposition of any product or part thereof, by TCL or any direct or indirect supplier or vendee or other transferee of TCL.

I. Waiver

Neither this Agreement nor any provision hereof may be waived without the prior written consent of the Party against whom such waiver is asserted. No delay or omission by either Party to exercise any right or power shall impair any such right or power to be construed to be a waiver thereof. Consent by either Party to, or waiver of, a breach by the other Party shall not constitute consent to, waiver of, or excuse for any other different or subsequent breach.

J. Assignment

Neither this Agreement nor any license or rights hereunder, in whole or in part, shall be assignable or otherwise transferable by either Party without the written consent of the other Party. Any attempt to do so in contravention of this Article shall be void and of no force and effect.

K. Notice

All notices, requests, demands, consents, agreements, and other communications required or permitted to be given under this Agreement shall be in writing and shall be: (a) delivered personally; (b) mailed to the Party to whom notice is given, by first class mail, postage prepaid; or (c) sent by facsimile or electronically, properly addressed with a confirmation copy to the Party's legal department (as appropriate) as follows:

Royalty reports in.xls format shall be emailed to: ipr.unit@ericsson.com.

Unless otherwise specifically provided for in this Agreement, such communications shall take effect upon receipt by the addressee, provided such communications shall be deemed to have arrived upon the expiration of seven (7) days from the date of sending in the case of registered or certified mail and on the day of receipt of the sender's facsimile confirmation of the transmission in the case of telefax.

The above addresses and contacts can be changed by providing notice to the other Party in accordance with this Clause.

L. Confidentiality

Except as may otherwise be required by law or as reasonably necessary for performance of this Agreement, each Party shall keep any information, whether of a commercial or technical nature including but not limited to any related reports, furnished by the other Party pursuant to this Agreement confidential. The confidentiality obligations hereunder shall, for ten (10) years, survive the expiration of this Agreement for any reason.

M. Headings

All headings used in this Agreement are inserted for convenience only and are not intended to affect the meaning or interpretation of this Agreement or any clause or provision herein.

Appendix C

Selected SDO IPR Policies

Below is a list of links to patent policies of existing SDOs that are publicly available. The policies referenced in this list are not necessarily representative of all of the clauses included in this Guide. Please note that SDO policies change frequently, and the links listed below may not contain the most recent versions of the relevant SDO policies.

ANSI	https://www.ansi.org/american-national-standards/ans-introduction/essential-requirements overview.aspx?menuid=3
ATIS	https://www.atis.org/policy/patent-policy/
Bluetooth	https://www.bluetooth.com/about-us/governing-documents/
Broadband Forum	https://www.broadband-forum.org/about-bbf/how-we-work/policies-procedures/intellectual-property-policy
CEA	https://cea-accredit.org/about-cea/policies-and-procedures =
ETSI	https://www.etsi.org/intellectual-property-rights
IEC/ISO	https://www.iec.ch/members_experts/tools/patents/patent_policy.htm
IEEE	https://standards.ieee.org/about/policies/index.html

IETF	https://www.ietf.org/standards/ipr/
INCITS	https://www.incits.org/standards-information/legal-info#:~:text=Patent%20Policy&text=INCITS%20encourages%20disclosure%2C%20where%20possible,with%20the%20ANSI%20Patent%20Policy.
ITU	https://www.itu.int/en/ITU-T/ipr/Pages/policy.aspx
JEDEC	https://www.jedec.org/about-jedec/patent-policy
OASIS	https://www.oasis-open.org/policies-guidelines/
OMA	https://omaspecworks.org/about/intellectual-property-rights/#:~:text=All%20OMA%20members%20operate%20under%20the%20same%20IPR%20policy.&text=Each%20Open%20Mobile%20Alliance%20member,the%20prepared%20or%20published%20specification.
SDA	https://www.sdcard.org/pdf/SDA_License_Agreement.pdf
TIA	https://tiaonline.org/what-we-do/standards/procedures-guidelines/
VESA	https://www.vesa.org/wp-content/uploads/2017/03/VP200D.pdf
VITA	https://www.vita.com/resources/Documents/Policies/vso-pp-r2d8.pdf
W3C	https://www.w3.org/Consortium/Patent/

Index

I

J

K

L